This book is a must read for every woman, especially in these times. We see ourselves in some aspects of the stories, and now we have real life strategies to motivate us and potentially help solve our dilemmas.

—Sharilyn J. Whitley

Magnificent, the content was raw, just the way I like it! Also . . . I need that workbook NOW!

—Karine Miller

I loved the featured stories and the approach Patrice took to solving real problems we, as women, face while balancing life.

—Tryna Kochanek

The humor threaded throughout the book eases the discomfort of facing the woman in the mirror!

—Fiona Rus

It's a pleasurable and valuable read. There were instant applications for me! I liked the transparency in the narratives.

—Beneatha Barkley

I enjoyed each of the personal stories. I could relate to each one in some shape or form. I especially enjoyed the quizzes. This book helps us [women] focus on us and not someone else's scenario or the so-called perfect picture other books often paint. There was raw and real material, and it was evident in every page.

—Nichole Griffin

The realness of the stories is great! Each relatable story reminds you of a girlfriend you have.

—Debra Lewis

Loved the pure honesty and witty delivery. Women from all walks of life can relate to the stories. This is a must read!

—Toni Smith

ARE YOU POLISHED?

ARE YOU POLISHED?

PAMPER YOURSELF
FIND YOUR RHYTHM
LIVE LIFE IN ABUNDANCE

PATRICE L. HARRIS

AUTHOR ACADEMY elite

Identifiers:
Library of Congress Control Number: 2020900807
ISBN: 978-1-64746-118-8 (paperback)
ISBN: 978-1-64746-119-5 (hardback)
ISBN: 978-1-64746-120-1 (ebook)

Available in paperback, hardback, e-book, and audiobook

Cover design and illustrations by Ms. Lacey Studios, LLC

Perfectly Polished, LLC Cleveland, OH
http://www.thepolishedjourney.com

perfectly POLISHED
ENTERPRISE

DEDICATIONS

Thank you, thank you, thank you, Daddy God. You wouldn't let the vision die, and you wouldn't let me let go. I dedicate my life, my ministry, and this book to you and the life you've called me to live.

To my hubby, Michael: you are more than I prayed, hoped, and waited for. You are my answered prayer. Thank you for releasing me and for pushing me forward. I pray God continues to enlarge my womb to help carry that which HE has called you to. MUAH!

To my mommy a.k.a. my inspiration to get and stay polished: thank you for holding my hand while admonishing me to put on my big girl panties, steady myself, and face this big world…fabulously. You are my #1 ladybug.

To my daddy: thank you for always believing in me and for representing the kind of man that would love and honor me. You made it impossible for the average man to capture my heart.

To Grandma Hattie: thank you for allowing me to be your brat. (I remember holding your face in my hands so you wouldn't look at anyone else.) Although you left this earthly realm a long time ago, I think of you daily. Thank you for always being stylish, wearing those big hats, and being poised, graceful, and beautiful. Above all, thank you for making sure I had a personal, intimate relationship with Jesus.

To my brother, Patrick: you are my twin. I know you're a Marine and can kill a man 18 different ways with your bare hands, but you're still my baby brother.

To the rest of the men in my family, Uncle Billy (I miss you so much), Uncle Jimmy, and Uncle Jerry (I love you both eternity times eternity), and Uncle June (you are my uncle, my brother, and at times, my other dad): you guys picked up the torch my dad set afire and spoiled me; some would even say I'm ruined.

To Yvette, my sister-in-love: thank you for being a true sister to me and for having three beautiful kids for me.

To all of my aunties, Aunt Sylvia, Aunt Minnie, Aunt Pegge, Auntie Janice, Auntie Mickie, Auntie Carol Ann, and Auntie Bird: you beautiful ladies have enriched my life to the max. Aunt Pegge, thank you for imparting the importance of soft hands, pedicured feet, and minding my own business; you will always be the epitome of a polished woman.

To Pastor and Mrs. Glover, Mrs. Deadwyler, Mrs. Taylor, Auntie Mary Bowen, and Mother Stone: thank you for watering the spiritual seeds Grandma Hattie planted. Thank you for all your prayers, guidance, and rebuke. I needed it.

To my spiritual parents, Pastor and Lady Vernon: you have been the Godly example I prayed for. Thank you for encouraging me and for admonishing me to stay faithful when I had come to the very end of me. Thank you for loving me and disciplining me all at the same time.

To my sistas/cousins/friends: Stephanie and Stacey, thank you for letting me tag along and always receiving me as I am. Thank you for encouraging me to "get polished" when I just wanted to give up. We've matured together, and I thank God for allowing me to travel this road with you. Toni, you are the bomb . . . tick . . . tick . . . BOOM! Your grace and faithful trust in Him are evident. Your straightforward, tell-it-like-it-is approach is hilarious and refreshing. Nikki, uhm, thank you for convincing me a little man lived under your stairs and for teaching me my first joke, ". . . John-John, I want my chitterlings." We were hilarious. Alana and Meleika, I know you're grown, but you're still my babies . . . act accordingly and do what I say please!

A special THANK YOU to every fearless, bold woman who selflessly shared her story with me so that many would be blessed.

To every woman who reads this book, please know you are fearfully and wonderfully made. May you be encouraged to not only get polished and live the life you deserve, but may you also take hold of God's hand and, in total trust, embrace His perfect will for your life.

Thank you, Ms. Lauren, for sticking with me all these years. God has given you such a gift! You pulled the images out of my head and brought them to life—I thank you from the bottom of my heart. Thank you, Nailah, for being my first editor and for pushing me to write better. Helen, you are a beast at what you do! (Oops, I used another exclamation mark.) You helped me see myself as a true author. You are invaluable! (I did it again.)

We will either change
our minds, thoughts,
values, and beliefs,
or change our behavior.

CONTENTS

PART I: UNDERSTANDING YOUR POLISHED TYPE

PART II: THE POLISHED JOURNEY

PART III: YOUR JOURNEY STARTS HERE

PART IV: ONE LAST THING

FOREWORD

In 2008, I had a conversation with the woman who ended up being the love of my life. During that conversation, we talked about goals and dreams, and that was the first time I heard about *Are You Polished?* As a man, the way this woman talked about her concept made me want to step up my game when it came to taking care of myself. In January 2010, my life changed forever. I married the woman God made just for me. She was, is, and will forever be the woman of my dreams.

Babe, I've watched you at your very best and we've walked through some very low times as well, but you faced both with grace and poise. From our wedding day to the loss of family members, and promotions to miscarriages, I've watched you go through with strength, dignity, and God's grace. I am so honored and proud you are my wife, friend, and lover. You are an example of a Proverbs 31 woman, as well as an example of God's goodness.

Over the years, you've written version after version of this book, and you passionately did so with determination while praying and asking God for clarity and direction. You wrote with excitement and great expectation, and yet with resolved disappointment, there were moments you walked away from your assignment. I'm so glad your desire to improve, encourage, and change the lives of everyone that reads this book overpowered your fears, insecurities, and self-doubt while writing it.

I love you, Patrice L. Harris. Your husband,
MICHAEL D. HARRIS

FROM THE AUTHOR

Initially, this book was my tongue-in-cheek attempt to encourage busy women to pamper themselves more often. I know what it's like to be burnt out and sick of everything and everybody. As I have been blessed with the gift of humor (trust me on this one), I figured there were other women for whom laughter is the medicinal marijuana that alleviates whatever stress life has bestowed upon them.

So, I set out to write a short, funny book of encouraging stories and anecdotes. I soon sensed God didn't exactly agree with my plan and my short, funny book became a labor-of-love along with acts of obedience, seasons of intense pain, rejection and isolation and now, prayerfully, my gift to you. You see, I wasn't allowed to simply write a cute book. I experienced being overwhelmed, overextended, overdrawn and underappreciated. I listened to tons and tons of women share their stories and their fight to get and remain *polished*.

I included a lot in this book (transparent stories, a self-assessment, experiential activities, pages to capture your perspective, basic action planning to motivate you forward, and more), because as my Grandma Hattie would say, "There is more than one way to skin a cat!" You don't have to do it all, but you will get the most out of this experience if you do. Have you ever read a great book that included what is clearly life-changing content and strategies, or quotes and statements that caused your spirit to leap, but you were still left asking:

But, HOW do I do that?
What steps do I follow?

How do I translate this to my life and situation?

I wrote this book in a manner that allows you the time and space to work through your thoughts and reactions, as well as the content and strategies provided. Again, you do not have to work through every exercise or answer every question, but it is recommended. If you are left with additional questions or wanting to dig deeper . . . I got you. That's what the workbook and journal are for.

If you are reading this, I trust you too have an interest in self-care and establishing a life *rhythm* that is perfect for you (whatever that may look like). I will not promise you will find perfect, everlasting peace and serenity as a result of reading this book and pampering yourself more than you do now. However, I do expect you to be encouraged to move forward on your journey. I do expect you to read with pen in hand and to write your reactions directly on the pages of this book, to highlight those statements that evoke your own ideas and strategies, and to earmark those pages that speak to your spirit. I expect you to be angry with me at moments, to laugh out loud, and yes, even stain some pages with tears, coffee, tea or bourbon (no judgment here).

Are You Polished? is based on my personal hypothesis: A woman's sanity is directly linked to her pedicure. I wrote this book to encourage busy, over-extended women all over the world to safely put themselves first by pampering themselves more often, finding their rhythm, and living life abundantly.

As you read *Are You Polished?*, work through the workbook, attend a Polished Party™, or utilize any of our custom tools and resources, do not compare your journey with anyone else's. Instead, relax and discover. Take whatever strategies you can use to help you along your path and pass them along to your family and friends. Above all, enjoy yourself and commit to the best thing you've got going . . . YOU!

DID YOU KNOW?

Women multi-task far more efficiently than men could ever even imagine. I bet you already knew that. Everyone knows that. But did you know that statistically, women experience more negative effects of stress and are more likely than men to report that our stress levels are on the rise? We are also much more likely than men to report physical and emotional symptoms of stress.

From CEOs and entrepreneurs, to politicians and domestic engineers, women have long embraced our roles as caretakers, nurturers, supporters, wives, moms, daughters, and friends. Somehow, we have also embraced the idea that what we do for our families and communities comes without a thank you, reward, or expectation to be pampered. (My husband would like me to acknowledge that Mother's Day is far more celebrated than Father's Day. Duly noted, dear.)

Let's take a look at a few statistics presented by the American Psychological Association:

- Women are more likely than men (28% vs. 20%) to report having a great deal of stress (8, 9 or 10 on a 10-point scale).

- Women are more likely to report that money (79% compared with 73% of men) and the economy (68% compared with 61% of men) are sources of great stress.

- Women are more likely to report physical and emotional symptoms of stress than men, such as having had a headache (41% vs. 30%), having felt as though they could cry (44% vs. 15%), or having had an upset stomach or indigestion (32% vs. 21%).

- 49% of women have lain awake at night because of stress; only 33% of women report being successful in their efforts to get enough sleep.

- 35% of women report success in their efforts to manage stress.

- 36% of women report success in their efforts to eat healthily.

- 29% of women report success in their efforts to be physically active.

To further illustrate the connection between stress and our holistic health, the Huffington Post published the following physical and emotional symptoms of stress that affect women:

1. Reduced Sex Drive	7. Insomnia
2. Irregular Periods	8. Weight Gain
3. Acne Breakouts	9. Decreased Fertility
4. Hair Loss	10. Increased Risk of Heart Disease and Stroke
5. Poor Digestion	
6. Depression	

Acne? Hair loss? Weight gain and reduced sex drive? These effects suck. They do, however, highlight a very sobering truth; ladies, we must take better care of ourselves. In light of these staggering facts about stress, the premise of this book is to encourage you to pamper yourself more frequently and to embrace a well-deserved life that best suits you.

Are You Polished? is an array of personal and witty stories told by women of varied backgrounds. It explores the hypothesis:

A woman's sanity is directly linked to her pedicure.

Wait! Before you respond, look down . . . is your pedicure perfectly polished? Or are your toes revealing a secret? You really do have one last nerve, and your boss, significant other, children, and parents have found it.

Although the explored hypothesis speaks to a woman's "sanity," this book does not address nor should be used to deal with real mental health issues. My intent is to encourage women to safely put themselves first and to pursue a sense of "balance" or *rhythm*. I placed the word balance in quotations mostly to invoke a common understanding of equilibrium, stability, and rest. I don't believe true balance is achievable, and certainly not sustainable.

Two common definitions of balance include "an even distribution of weight enabling someone or something to remain upright and steady," and "a condition in which different elements are equal or in the correct proportions." Although we make every effort to remain upright and steady as we juggle all of our different tasks and responsibilities, we all know these definitions are not realistic in our very real worlds. If the condition of your pedicure, your edges, or your last nerve reflect failed attempts to give everything and everyone 100% of you, then you know we cannot assign multiple areas of our lives the same weight, value, or level of importance at the same time—at least not for very long.

I do believe, however, we each have a rhythm that is as unique as our thumbprints, and is the required code to unlock peace, stability and rest. Rhythm is defined as "a strong, regular, repeated pattern of movement or sound." In other words, I believe each of us must find and establish strong, regularly repeated patterns that move us forward, towards our goals. Throughout this book, the words balance and rhythm are used interchangeably to reference this concept of stability and forward movement, whatever that may look like for you. Have you ever felt overwhelmed by the lists of things to do or the weight of being the go-to woman? Or perhaps you have confronted the possibility of your dreams quickly drifting away and have questioned, "Where has the fabulous ME gone?" Have you ever wondered how to hold on to your sanity and look sane at the same time? Have you ever fantasized about escaping to some faraway place where no one knows your name or asks you to do one flipping thing? Even if you faintly responded "yes" to any of these scenarios, *Are You Polished?* is the one true accessory you need to complement your hectic life.

This book looks at several types of "polished" women and is divided into four sections:

i. **Understanding Your Polished Type:** includes a quick self-assessment designed to give you insight into what type of polished woman you may be currently.

ii. **The Polished Journey:** highly personal, entertaining, and sometimes heart-breaking stories of women, plus their advice on (a) what/who you may need to *unpack* in order to make room for your true essentials, (b) what/who you may need to *pack* along your journey toward becoming polished, and (c) how to maintain and nurture your polished status. Finally, each woman answers seven polished questions to give you even greater insight into their strategy and journey.

iii. **Your Polished Journey Starts Here:** strategies that help you determine what areas of your life may need to be polished up and in what order. This section helps you start your own polished journey.

iv. **One Last Thing:** your polished bonus track. Sections 1–3 of this book ensure you are positioned to capture the abundant life you deserve. This final section highlights best practices that help you along your polished journey and keep you moving forward.

Come on, join the *Are You Polished?* movement. Laugh, cry, get angry, and get healed with us as we test the hilarious hypothetical connection between a woman's sanity and her pedicure. Join an elite group of women who not only know the secret meaning behind the question, "Are you polished?" but also know the tenacious plight of getting polished.

INTRODUCTION

Growing up, I was surrounded by *strong* women. They were everywhere. My mother didn't take crap from anyone. She once chased my school bully in her long, white Cadillac, got out the car, and slapped him in the face with her red leather glove. Man, I love that woman.

My grandmother laundered clothes for a living, frequently trained younger men to be her supervisor, and made some of the most beautiful clothing designs on the weekends. My Auntie Janis was the perfect amalgamation of elegance, poise, creativity, and her colorful phrases of profanity. She was hilarious.

Then, there was a host of aunties who collectively exposed me to the historic Karamu House in Cleveland, Ohio, evoked a love for dramatic dance, and taught me the value of my own opinion: "If that is what YOU want, then get it!" My Auntie Carol Ann inspired my revelation that nothing can happen that a high-speed car drive with the windows down, the radio blasting and me singing at the top of my voice won't fix. "Girls, they wanna . . . they wanna have fun . . . they wanna . . . ! They wanna have . . . just a' wanna, just a' wanna . . . ah—ah!"

I remember thinking I couldn't wait for me and my cousins to become what my mom and her sisters refer to as G.A.W.s (grown *bleep* women); the ladies in our lives made it look so easy. Yes, they experienced stress, hard times, and difficult seasons, but they were always well dressed, well groomed, sweet-smelling, and . . . well . . . polished.

THE QUESTION: ARE YOU POLISHED?

After a few ill-fitting training bras, ill-advised relationships, and a sizable number of major fashion faux pas, my cousins and I grew up. Over the years, I noticed that several of the strong women around us weren't always polished. Sometimes, they were stressed out, and acted and looked as crazy as shot possums. As my cousins and I were coming into our own and defining "polished" for ourselves, it became painfully clear that life was hard—often unfair—and maintaining a sense of self was a lot of work. Exactly how was I supposed to be one of the prettiest belles at the ball, maintain a brick house body, sport the latest hairstyle, ensure my nails and toes were perfectly manicured, wear the latest fashions, acquire multiple degrees, start a business, get on the corporate fast-track, get married, have 2.5 children, write a book, go into ministry, make a difference in some foreign country as an evangelist, home-school my kids, travel the world, and learn how to cook without losing my flipping mind?

I filled my plate with experiences and responsibilities that were an expansion of what I saw lived out in front of me, all the while trying to maintain my own polished-ness. *If that is what you want, then get it.* Over time, my cousins and I learned the more hectic life became, the more the condition of our pedicures devolved from fabulous to plain ol' rough. This observation seemed to be true for us and many other women.

Sometimes we would try and guess the condition of a woman's pedicure based on how she looked, acted, or responded to the situations around her. For example, if we saw two mothers in a store with their children, and one mom seemed to have a handle on her kids, was laughing with her little ones, and was visibly relaxed, while the other mom seemed stressed out and was threatening her children, while her hair sat on the top of her head like a bird's nest, we would guess that the first mom was polished. Meaning, the first mom's polished pedicure reflects her ability to juggle her responsibilities and self-care.

As for the second mom, we would guess she—along with her pedicure and her stress management skills—was a hot mess.

My cousins and I developed our own language to secretly describe the degree to which we were successfully juggling everything on our plates. Whether in person or over the phone, our response had to be immediate whenever we heard, *"Are you polished?"* Likewise, the translation of our response communicated more than the typical, "I'm doing well" or "I'm *so* busy."

THE RESPONSES

The simple *are you polished* question allowed us to check in with one another without intruding too much or requiring a lengthy conversation around the often-seedy details of whatever situation we found ourselves in. Truth be told, just hearing the question often made us laugh hysterically at the thought of the answer and the seedy details. Although we linked our secret salutation to our pedicures, our response said everything, and sometimes even launched a call to action.

So, if I ask you, "Are you polished?" there are several ways you could respond based on the definitions my cousins and I created. If you respond:

- **I'm Polished!** You mean . . . I am juggling all my current responsibilities, managing stress in a healthy manner, and consistently taking time to pamper myself and ensure my pedicure is on point.

- **I'm Layered!** You mean . . . a lot is going on, and I am starting to feel the pressure and stress of juggling all of my current responsibilities. Although I haven't made much time for myself or the maintenance of my pedicure, at least I look good and so do my toes. I had just enough time to add a few fresh coats of paint to them. However, this is a heads-up that I may need your help if I don't get a handle on things soon.

- **I'm Chipped!** You mean . . . I dropped the ball on a few things . . . namely *me*. Not only is my polish starting to chip away, so too is my peace and sanity. I have no time for me. I am officially stressed and stretched out. I need a little help. Talk me through this, encourage me, and remind me I'm fabulous.

- **I'm wrecked!** You just said . . . HELP! Everything has fallen through the cracks, including me. I have nothing left for anyone or anything. I've let go completely. 9-1-1—come get me!

- **I'm High Polished!** You mean . . . it's all about me right now. Everything and everyone else can catch me if they can. What stress? Too much faith in others leads to disappointment, so I don't depend on anyone outside of myself. I'm my own best chick. My hair, my nails, my lashes, my clothes, and my toes are on point. I deserve it all . . . all the time.

BUT WHY THE PEDICURE?

You may be wondering why the pedicure is significant to a woman's sanity. Of course, there are other tell-tale signs that a woman has given too much of herself and is running on fumes. Perhaps she has lost her sense of humor or her desire to keep her hair done, or heaven forbid, you can't remember the last time she smelled like anything more than the last meal she cooked. Maybe the tell-tale sign is her string of failed relationships, her inability to grasp the concept that credit card debt must be repaid, or her addiction to exercise (I wish), food, or sex (my husband wishes). Aside from the observations made growing up, the pedicure was chosen as the correlation between a woman's sanity and her well-being because of the following:

- Your pedicure is often covered; therefore, it is the easiest thing to neglect and hide.

- A pedicure is obtainable for everyone. You can give yourself a pedicure at home if necessary.

- A pedicure requires more time than a basic manicure. Amid a hectic schedule, dedicated time and concerted effort are needed to maintain your pedicure.

- The time it takes to get a pedicure could qualify as *pampering* time and is enough time to clear your head.

Still not convinced? Trust me. If you see a woman whose hair is a mess and she's talking to herself *and* responding, know that she stopped taking care of her pedicure a long time ago. (Again, I am not talking about our sisters with legitimate mental health challenges; I am addressing those of us who put in less effort toward self-care as more and more stress piles on.)

INVESTIGATING THE HYPOTHESIS

Patrice, Stephanie is on the phone.
Hello?
Hey! How are you doing?
I'm okay . . .
Uhm, *are you polished?*
. . . (wait) . . .(wait) . . . Nope.
Okay, I'll check on you a little later. You know God loves you, and everything will be okay, right?
. . . (wait) . . . (wait) . . . Yep.

It had been two weeks since I'd called off my wedding before I was asked *that* question.

The next day, Stephanie showed up. She forced me to get out of the bed, take a shower (I had showered in those two weeks, just not that day or the day before), put on some cute clothes, and simply talk while she listened. We eventually landed in a state of hysteria as we recounted all the jokes we'd told over the years about other folks, their pedicures and craziness. It was pretty humorous to realize even we had stumbled under the pressures of life and had fallen off the sanity wagon a few times.

In the weeks prior, I barely had enough strength and energy to comb the front section of my hair. (Who was looking at the back of my head anyway?) Sleep, breakfast, work, sleep. That was my routine. I couldn't get past the moment. I didn't know where to start, and I didn't know what to stop. My mind wouldn't rest. I remember asking myself, *without this relationship, how does my personal image change? Is there still purpose and ministry inside of me? Will I ever get married? Will I ever have my 2.5 children? If I don't go to Africa as a missionary, who will? What the heck am I supposed to write a book about?*

One day, the impact of the question hit me. *Are you polished?* No, I wasn't. Not only was my pedicure jacked up, but so too was my state of mind. I realized I didn't have the tools needed to navigate this life God had given me and become what I was purposed to become without giving too much of myself away. Was I going to succumb to the stress of it all and become a part of the statistics? *Did I really sit on the couch and try to plan time to have a nervous breakdown?* I did. But after a while, that required too much thought, so I settled on driving down the highway in the middle of the night with my eyes closed, hoping I would run off the road. *STOP! Somebody, anybody, come get my crazy, un-polished, grown bleep.*

I spent the next several years trying to understand what "polished" meant for me. I tried to lay hold of it and even fake it, but I sulked into depression when I thought it was unattainable for me. I encouraged others to pursue it, went to nail salons regularly, and gave myself pedicures when my money was funny. I spent quiet time with my thoughts and learned to appreciate me. More importantly, I developed an intimate relationship with God and spent a lot of time listening to the stories of other women who had dreams of their own and a take-no-prisoners fight in their bellies.

I learned two things during that time: (1) I had to define what polished looked like for me, and (2) the degree to which I was polished was based on my ability to effectively manage *me*—my whole person, not only my toes, or job, or relationships. This revelation led to five major categories with which I define the term polished:

- Emotional & Spiritual

- Self-Identity

- Physical

- Relational

- Financial

Consistency was the key. I found that if I regularly spent quality time on each of these categories, it was easier to maintain a higher level of self. On the contrary, if I let any category become overwhelming or neglected, my sanity and perfectly polished pedicure soon showed signs of wear and tear. While committed to working on me, I faced one of my greatest heartbreaks and almost lost my mental grip. I wondered if the connection between my sanity—the degree to which I managed stress, purposefully pampered myself, and pursued a sense of stability—and my pedicure was uniquely mine, or did other women share in this phenomenon? To test my hypothesis, I set out to ask as many women as possible, *"Are you polished?"*

The hypothesis: A woman's sanity is directly linked to her pedicure.

The conclusion: I don't know if there is a direct correlation, but I thought it would be a worthy, adventurous, hilarious-at-best journey to pursue.

Before you respond, look down at your toes.

PART ONE

UNDERSTANDING YOUR POLISHED TYPE

TELL THE TRUTH...I DARE YOU!

Knowing yourself is the beginning of all wisdom.

—Aristotle

So, are you polished? Obviously, this is not an entire book about your pedicure and the assumption you're automatically fifty shades of crazy if your toes are absent of nail polish. Nor am I suggesting that nail polish is the cure-all for a manic life. I mentioned it before, but it is worth mentioning again that the intent of this book is neither to address nor treat serious mental health issues. This book, however, is my attempt to encourage you to pamper yourself, live life in abundance, and actively pursue balance or rhythm (whatever that looks like for you) in every aspect of your life.

Part I of *Are You Polished?* provides a quick, fun self-assessment designed to provide insight into the polished woman you may be currently. The assessment categorizes several polished types and concludes with a description of each. Take the assessment, then follow along as a few women describe their journeys in Part II.

THE ASSESSMENT

R ead each question or statement. Provide your honest, immediate response by selecting the answer that most accurately describes your **current** situation. To break a tie between answers, select the answer that describes you most often. Use the scoring tool at the end of the assessment to determine your polished type.

1. If I were asked today, "What do you want to be when you grow up?" I would answer:

   A. I want to be _____, and I'm actively working toward that goal right now (and/or have accomplished what I set out to achieve).

   B. I still want to be _____; I have started and stopped working on this goal many times, but it's still very important to me.

   C. I used to want to be _____, but I don't know how I'm going to get it all done. Right now, I don't have time to daydream.

   D. I am exactly what I want to be—fabulous, baby!

   E. I don't know.

2. In my most recent relationship:

   A. We set time aside for date night as well as our individual time away from each other.

   B. We spend as much time together as we can, when we can.

   C. We barely spend any intimate time together.

   D. He adjusts to my schedule.

   E. I take whatever time he has available.

3. A significant other is:

   A. Someone to partner with to accomplish common goals or a shared vision.

   B. Someone I can help accomplish their goals and vision; I was built for this.

   C. More work than I can handle right now.

   D. Someone who will pamper me.

   E. Someone who will rescue me.

4. I wear clothes that:

   A. Compliment my shape, communicate my personality, and are appropriate for the occasion.

   B. Communicate my role, responsibilities, and importance. Looking the part is important to me.

   C. Are comfortable and easy to wash and go.

   D. Push it up, tuck it in, and show 'em off. If you got it, flaunt it.

   E. Are dark or neutral in color, loose fitting, and comfortable. I hate ironing.

5. My budget is:

   A. Created, checked on a regular basis (weekly and monthly), and followed to the tee.

   B. Created, checked periodically (every other month or trimester) and followed as closely as possible.

   C. Too time-consuming. Maintenance requires too much time, so it's not up to date.

   D. A list of income avenues, sponsors, or *suga-daddies*. Maintaining my budget doesn't require real work.

   E. Non-existent.

6. When it comes to stress management:

   A. I can handle a lot—one thing at a time.

   B. I can handle it all; I secretly enjoy the challenge.

   C. It has become too much, both the stress and trying to manage it.

   D. I don't deal with a lot of stress; I simply ignore it.

   E. Everything seems to be stressful right now.

7. Whenever I feel depressed, my first reaction is to:

   A. Take a moment and reflect on how blessed I am.

   B. Take control of something/anything (e.g., work, budget, etc.).

   C. Do whatever made me feel better the last time (e.g., eating, shopping, gossiping, etc.).

    D. Demand some quality ME time (e.g., buy ME something, get MY hair or nails done, hang around people that tell ME how fabulous I am, etc.).

    E. Do nothing. It'll pass one day.

8. To become/maintain the vision I have for myself, I:

    A. Revisit my vision/goals often and consistently work toward bringing them to fruition.

    B. Revisit my vision/goals when I have downtime. Sometimes, I get sidetracked and have to redirect my efforts toward my goals.

    C. Think about what I could do all the time; I just don't have time to do it.

    D. Check my nails, check my hair, check my clothes, and check my shoes. Am I missing something?

    E. Vision? I can barely see past today.

9. My family and friends come to me:

    A. For support and encouragement, but sometimes I have to say no.

    B. Too often, but I get it; I make things happen.

    C. Too often; I'm starting to resent being the go-to gal.

    D. Because I am the life of the party; I'm a good time.

    E. Mostly to check on me.

10. My credit score is:

A. Between 720–800. I've worked hard to get here, and I'm still working hard to maintain it.

B. Improving. I got a little busy and let a few things slip through the cracks. It happens, but I'm working on it.

C. Uhm, I'm not sure. I haven't had time to check it in a while.

D. Must be good. I keep getting new cards.

E. I don't know; it's not important.

11. My strategy for my personal time:

A. Includes at least 30 minutes daily, a planned weekly pampering event, and a planned annual vacation.

B. Is slowly fading, but I try to recoup often. I pamper myself when my schedule allows or when I start to look a little crazy (even if I must add a few coats of nail polish myself).

C. Non-existent. I get in wherever I fit in. Besides, right now I don't have time to plan my personal time.

D. Is all about me—all day, every day. I take care of me first, then everything else falls into place.

E. Does not exist. (What is this *strategy* you speak of?) Even the thought of an elaborate strategy makes my head hurt.

12. My family and friends:

A. Know about and respect my quiet time and planned pampering time.

B. Depend on me to take care of things. I am the go-to person.

C. Are starting to complain they don't see me enough. My schedule has become so hectic, I'm not available like I used to be.

D. Think that I am the life of the party, but they know not to ask me to do too much.

E. Don't spend a lot of time around me, but when they see me, sometimes they'll ask how they can assist me.

13. I see myself as:

A. Wonderfully made, although I have some areas of improvement I am actively working on.

B. Superwoman sometimes. I am my happiest when I am busy.

C. A woman in need. I need a break, a vacation, and a drink. I don't see a way out sometimes.

D. The center of attention, although I sometimes feel hidden.

E. How do I see myself? Now that's a hard question. "Broken," is my best answer.

14. I currently eat:

A. A pre-planned breakfast, lunch, dinner, and two snacks every day.

B. At least two to three times per day—something quick and easy.

C. When I can, but I often snack and eat out.

D. A cereal bar, a couple of shakes, and whatever I order on dinner dates.

E. All the time, OR not often enough.

15. My long-term vision for my finances:

   A. Focuses on financing my retirement. I know exactly how much I need to retire comfortably and stay retired. I am working toward that goal now.

   B. Is coming together. I have a few avenues to pursue financial security, and I am currently pursuing all possibilities.

   C. Focuses on paying all my bills this month.

   D. Includes enough money or credit to get everything I want right now.

   E. Is blurred. Thinking about it causes too much stress.

16. If I ranked my relationships right now, I would rank myself:

   A. First, so that I can be helpful to others.

   B. First, along with everyone else. My responsibilities as a wife, mother, daughter, aunt, employee, etc. are equal with me. I give everything, including myself, 100%.

   C. Maybe second or third after I make sure everyone is taken care of.

   D. Numeral Uno. Are you kidding me? Of course, I come first.

   E. I don't have the energy to make anything a priority.

17. If my emotions were a rollercoaster, you would:

    A. Laugh, cry, scream, and shout equally. You would also appreciate the safety features; this ride takes frequent breaks to reboot and let disgruntled passengers off.

    B. Probably think this ride is not the most exciting ride. It won't get too crazy because of the amount of people watching, but you'll get your money's worth. This ride never stops.

    C. Think this ride is crazy. Put your safety belt on, *suga*. You are in for the ride of your life.

    D. Mostly go uphill with a few low dips. But don't worry, the valleys pass through hidden tunnels no one can see.

    E. Think this ride is pretty dull, unless you like long periods of spinning in circles and extremely low dips, only to be elevated to a flat, uneventful track.

18. The relationship between my past, the woman I am today, and the woman I am becoming is:

    A. Fluid. What I've learned from my past has helped me be the woman I am today, and I expect to get better with time.

    B. Consistent. When I think about it, I've always been a workaholic. Consistency is how I got here, and it's how I'll get to the next level.

    C. Disconnected. I'm not where I dreamed of being, and I lost sight of what I wanted.

D. Consistent. I have *always* focused on me. I was fabulous yesterday, I'm fabulous today, and I expect to be fabulous forever.

E. Dependent. I am who I am today because of what happened to me or what I've done in the past.

19. When I see other women who are physically attractive, I:

A. Am encouraged.

B. Feel competitive; I need to get on it and stay on it.

C. Feel jealous. She doesn't have to juggle all the things I have to juggle.

D. Think to myself, *she could do better.*

E. Get depressed.

20. Outside of a 401K at work, investments are:

A. A part of my diversified portfolio. My money is working for me.

B. Taken care of by Whitman, Whitman, and Whitman Financial Services; I read my quarterly reports when I can.

C. Confusing. I need to research how to invest. As soon as I get some extra money and time, I'll investigate.

D. 'Sponsors' that invest in my hair, nails, dinner, wardrobe, etc.

  E. A waste of time. I don't believe in taking chances with my money. Besides, who has the time or energy for that?

21. In my spare time, I:

  A. Have enough energy to enjoy volunteering at church, in my community, serving as a board member of a local organization, and/or spending time with my family and friends.

  B. Keep running. Even my spare time is busy.

  C. Can barely move. Whenever I happen to stumble into some spare time, I can be found staring out a window, watching TV, snoozing, or quietly planning my escape.

  D. Window shop or browse the latest fashion magazines while planning my next makeover.

  E. Don't know what to do with me. I have spare time, but I don't have spare energy.

22. When I stand naked in the mirror, I think:

  A. I love me some me! I may not be perfect, but I'm currently working toward my physical goals right now (or have acquired them).

  B. I have a lot on my plate right now, but I will not quit. I start my new health regimen next week.

  C. I'm used to it now. I may not be where I once wanted to be, but it's okay. You'll have to love me for me; it is what it is.

  D. Seriously, it doesn't get any better. Well, maybe if I had _____'s legs and _____'s hair.

14

E. Nothing. I stopped looking in the mirror and caring what it reflected a long time ago. It's easier this way; I avoid mirrors at all cost.

23. Peace is:

    A. Something I purposely seek daily.

    B. Something I schedule to attain frequently.

    C. Is a fond but distant memory.

    D. Too loud for me to enjoy.

    E. Not attainable nor realistic.

24. When it comes to my health:

    A. I know my numbers (i.e., systolic, diastolic, cholesterol, resting heart rate, and weight) and what they should be. I am actively maintaining healthy ranges in these areas.

    B. I get a physical every few years and know how much I should weigh.

    C. I haven't been to the doctor in a while. I don't feel my best, but it's only stress.

    D. I don't know my numbers, but I look good.

    E. I go (or should go) to the doctor often. I don't feel well, and I don't know my numbers.

25. If I were a bank:

    A. I would be a reliable, FDIC-approved institution from whom you could secure a significant loan.

    B. I would be a credible, FDIC-approved institution from whom you could acquire a small loan, but during limited hours. This institution would also be a laundromat, drive-through restaurant, cleaning service, chauffeuring service, and counseling office.

C. This institution wouldn't currently award loans of any amount; however, we would also operate as a laundromat, drive-through restaurant, cleaning service, chauffeuring service, and counseling office.

D. My institution wouldn't give loans, but you could invest.

E. My institution would be in default; however, it would be available for people to stop in to invest if they'd like. They would simply have to ignore the group of creditors gathered outside the door.

What Type of
Polished Woman
Are You?

Follow the directions to determine your score and your polished type:

Step One

Count how many questions/statements you answered with an *A* response and write that number in the first space provided for line *a*. Then, multiply that number by 4 points and write the total in the second space provided for line *a*.

For example, if you answered 3 questions with an *A* response, you would write 3 in the first space and 12 in the second space for line *a* (3 X 4 = 12).

Example:
a. # of *A*s _____ **3** X 4 points = **12**

Step Two

Repeat this process for lines *b* through *e*. (Multiply each number by the appropriate point value listed: 3, 2, 1, or 0.)

STEP THREE

Determine your total score by adding all your point values from lines *a* through *e*. Write the sum on the space provided for your total score.

a. # of *As*   X   4 points =

b. # of *Bs*   X   3 points =

c. # of *Cs*   X   2 points =

d. # of *Ds*   X   1 point =

e. # of *Es*   X   0 points =

TOTAL Score =

STEP FOUR

Use the scale below to determine your polished type. Then, find and read the appropriate description.

a. 91–100 points = Polished

b. 71–90 points = Layered

c. 51–70 points = Chipped

d. 25–50 points = High Polished

e. 0–24 points = Wrecked

a. Polished! (91–100 points)

This woman has found her rhythm and takes time to ensure her life is balanced (for her), vibrant, whole, joyful, healthy, and as stress-free as possible. How does she do this? By continuously assessing her stress levels and unpacking unnecessary drama in her life, like gossip, toxic relationships, etc. You may wonder how she does it all; she doesn't. The polished woman knows when to say no so that she can fully operate in excellence (instead of lack) when she says yes. This woman knows when to quietly slip away to spend a few self-indulgent moments by herself. She not only knows when to get away, but she also has dedicated time for herself, so she can be the blessing she is called to be when she returns to the role of wife, mommy, CEO, minister, daughter, auntie, neighbor, volunteer, or whatever hat she's wearing at that moment.

The polished woman is comfortable in her skin and has learned to live a life that is perfect for her. She enjoys this journey called life and looks forward to embracing the woman she's becoming. This woman's wisdom comes from knowing being polished doesn't merely happen overnight and stress is inevitable. Thus, this woman is open to new ideas and strategies to maintain her equilibrium. (Translation: keep reading because you might learn something today that you may need tomorrow.)

b. Layered (71–90 points)

This woman wants you to believe she is polished under the premise that if she *looks* polished, then she must be. But if you take a closer look, you will see she is juggling way too much. If you take a much closer look, you may find a woman more concerned with the appearance of it all. She might stay in a non-mutually beneficial relationship rather than face the fact her partner is not a part of her destiny. She might pretend she has it all together rather than pick up the phone and call Consumer Credit Counselors. You know this *layered* woman. She doesn't know when to say no and really piles it on. One man, ministry, or rescue mission after the next, and two or maybe three more assignments before she takes a break. This woman is always available to address someone else's issues.

She has no time to stop and no time for pampering. Merely add another layer and voila . . . it's like new.

Another class, another degree . . . can't stop now . . . another shade of red and no one will be able to tell she almost lost it. If this woman can add one more layer, she can still look polished. But wait, the new layers aren't lasting as long as they used to. They seem to be wearing off and wearing down. What can this layered woman do to save herself? This woman needs to learn to say no, embrace the power of slowing down, and come to terms with the fact that the *S* on her chest is fading.

c. Chipped (51–70 points)

This is what happens when the stress of not saying no has gone too far, when doing too much for too long becomes evident. The *chipped* woman is tired of pretending to have it together. She desperately tries to hold it all together, but pieces of what made her unique have started to chip away. Perhaps at first, it was her laughter or her knack for storytelling. Maybe her love for cooking has turned into an unhealthy soul-tie with food. Maybe much of what has chipped away she picked at and threw aside herself. For example, the guy was never right for her, or she wasn't good enough for him. The job chipped away. Her dreams chipped away. Be careful, this woman is on the edge. With a little encouragement, she may find her way back to the sanity of smooth heels and ten perfectly polished toes.

However, one more tug at her limited time, resources, or love and we may lose her to a wrecked world where rough feet with overgrown cuticles and hangnails are the norm and unpolished toenails scrape the ground. To put it simply, the chipped woman is the epitome of multitasking gone wild. The best next steps for the chipped woman are slow down; embrace one task and one assignment at a time.

d. High Polished (25–50 points)

Ms./Mrs./Miss Thang has it going on! Please do not get it twisted, she does not have a problem saying no to others so she can say yes to her favorite event . . . HERSELF. Yes, darling, this woman is an event. It takes more than a notion to get her hair coiffed ever-so-perfectly and to accomplish perfectly manicured and polished acrylics, gels, or whatever the new low-maintenance nail process is. It is no easy task to acquire flawless makeup every day. Is she going to work, church, or a gala? It doesn't matter. Her lashes flash brilliantly for all occasions. This *high polished* woman keeps a closely guarded secret; one you would never guess by looking at her. Is the secret that she is totally in love with herself? Nah, that's too easy. Is the secret that she always desires to be desired? Perhaps, we're getting closer. The high polished woman appears to be completely in love with herself and thrives on the consistent admiration of both men and women because . . . well . . . she's hurt. Keeping up with the latest trends and maintaining a high polished profile is not only a tiring project; it also hides a significant amount of disappointment, hurt, and distrust. If you look at this woman closely, you may see she's layered, chipped, or even financially wrecked. (There is a high price to pay to maintain a high polished status.) This woman is guarded, but if you're lucky enough to establish a meaningful relationship with her, she might relax enough to let her hair down (literally). The high polished woman may be self-centered, immature, or simply too hurt to focus again on others. The truth is, it's no one's business but her own. This fabulous woman could benefit from facing the root of her truth and slowly embracing the gift of vulnerability.

e. Wrecked (0–24 points)

The *wrecked* woman is more than tired of pretending. She is firmly planted in some surreal world where there is no pressure to be polished at all. She doesn't have to worry about saying no to others because no one is asking. Unfortunately, this woman is not taking care of herself. Maybe she was once a polished or even a high polished woman, but life happened to her again and again. Maybe she tried to hold it together in the beginning, but as more responsibilities, expectations and even disappointments began to pile on, she found it difficult to breathe. As time progressed and it became challenging to juggle it all, this woman began to lose her grip. Along with her grip, she lost her peace of mind. Left with no time or energy for self-preservation or volunteering, she quit her ministries, hasn't spoken to her girls in a while, and only has shadows of relationships in the background. Her performance at work, her smile, and her hopes for a better tomorrow have all faded away. On top of everything else, her polish wore off, and all that is left is a woman who (like her pedicure) is wholly exposed, callused, and run over. GET UP SIS. GET UP! It's easier said than done, but this beautiful sister needs to remind herself of how wonderful she really is. A strategy to pamper herself, get organized, and manage stress is the unlock she needs.

Your Perspective

 What did your assessment results reveal?

 What made you laugh?

 What made you cringe?

What else can you add to the description of your polished type?

PART TWO

THE POLISHED JOURNEY

UHM . . . ARE YOU POLISHED?

Every woman has a story. Listen with your whole heart.

—I said that

Are you polished, or do you need to get your polish together? Regardless of the type of polished woman each of us may be—and regardless of how we handle stress—we all have at least one thing in common: we all have a story to tell. Enjoy this next section as real women share the real stories of their polished journeys. These women are diverse in their ethnic backgrounds, socioeconomic statuses, religious and political affiliations, as well as their age, marital and motherhood statuses, and career choices. Each woman, however, has a story about her journey towards becoming her best possible self.

In Part II of *Are You Polished?*, these highly personal, entertaining, and sometimes heart-breaking stories outline (1) what/who you may need to *unpack* in order to make room for your true essentials, (2) what/who you may need to *pack* on your journey toward becoming polished, and (3) how to maintain and nurture your polished status and avoid those things we allow to take up too much time, space, physical and

27

emotional energy. Finally, each woman answers seven polished questions to give you even greater insight into their strategy and journey. These stories will make you cry, laugh, cuss, and of course, relate. When these women are done sharing their stories, you will want to share your story as well or begin your own polished journey. Either way, you won't be able to resist asking your girlfriends, *"Are you polished?"*

PATRICE

TRAINING AND DIVERSITY
EXECUTIVE

I used to think I could do it all. Whatever you need, yes, I can. I'm every woman. Haven't you seen the *S* on my chest? Sleep? No time for that. Rest? I'll get that when I'm dead and gone. Vacation? How about a staycation while I work on my house, start a new business, or write another book (although the last two aren't finished)? Somewhere along the way, I got too busy to take care of me. And as I mentioned before, I realized I didn't have the necessary tools to successfully navigate through this life.

I flirted with depression and resentment every 182 days like clockwork. Then that question began to nag me. "Are you polished?" Nope. I needed a change, so I tried to figure it all out. Over time, I made progress. I saw how I was maturing emotionally, how my relationships grew more supportive and rewarding, and how my financial aptitude was developing. I even embraced the changes my body went through as I matured. I was proud of myself and the level of polish I thought I had reached. As a newlywed, I may have been having too much fun (wink, wink), because I slowly began to add more to my plate. I added so much that I hadn't noticed I'd slipped from being polished to layered and was quickly descending into being chipped.

Despite my inability to maintain my sense of stability, I was glad I had already done some of the work, when life hit me again.

IT WAS THE BEST OF TIMES AND THE WORST OF TIMES

Over the span of twelve months, I was promoted to vice president at work, my husband went into ministry full-time, and we were both promoted to elders at our church. During that same twelve-month timeframe, I also had three miscarriages and major surgery to remove four cysts—one of which had developed, grown, and embedded itself into the muscle behind my uterus. (Translation: OUCH!)

I miscarried my second child while I was being promoted at work. Literally. I'm sure I appeared to be the most ungrateful person ever. There I was, sitting across from two Senior Vice Presidents as they outlined my accomplishments and why I was the logical choice for this newly created position, and all I could do was grimace because it felt like I had the worst menstrual cramps ever. I smiled and said I looked forward to the official promotion offer, then I bolted out of the room and ran to the bathroom. I was so thankful for the friend who held my hand as I called my husband and doctor once I got back to my office.

Later, my doctor apologized for my loss. "It's not your fault, you didn't push me down the stairs," I laughed. "God has a plan." My doctor encouraged me to try again since I was already 40—I wanted to punch her in the face. Despite taking several days to fully miscarry my baby, I went about my daily activities as usual. I went to work the next day, participated in a wedding on the following Saturday and ministered in church that Sunday. After my first lady (my pastor's wife) instructed me to grieve this loss, I sat on the altar, cried a little, and asked God to replace this baby with another.

A few months later, I was running full speed again. There were late nights and weekends at work, leadership or pulpit development trainings at church, with any other scraps of time belonging to my family. I was managing it all and I started to feel like myself again. I liked the tempo of busy, even though our home looked a little messy and our laundry piles were beginning to take on a life of their own. We hired a housekeeper to come in once a month . . . problem solved. After some time, I noticed my period was late. Unlike the jubilee with which I met my second pregnancy, this time I felt it may be an inconvenience. By now, I was a new vice president, responsible for three departments, and I wasn't sure I was going to continue to succeed at work and at being a brand new 40+ mom.

Campus liaisons? Late one night after a leadership meeting, our pastor and first lady met with me and my husband to inquire about our interest in managing a church campus one hour from our home. At the end of this meeting, my first lady admonished me to take a home pregnancy test (I was too afraid to do so). Off to CVS we went. Yes, yes, yes, I was pregnant. And yes, my husband accepted the role of part-time Campus Liaison. Fourteen hours later, in the same bathroom of my previous miscarriage at work, I felt that familiar cramping again. After a day or so, the dark brown spotting gave way to a bright red flow. Once again, my friend held my hand and encouraged me to take it easy this time. I knew the drill. I wore pads for the next week, cried a little, and prayed on the altar at church again asking God to replace this baby with another. This time, I didn't bother to call my physician. I knew what had happened, and there wasn't anything she could do.

I threw myself back into work and stood by my husband's side as he later accepted the Campus Liaison position full-time. I met with my direct reports and my teams. I played the corporate game and pushed myself (and everyone around me) to achieve goal after goal. All was well. All but the bills, the house, and our piles of clothes—I couldn't find anything, not even socks, so I simply bought us some more—more socks, more clothes, more shoes and more underwear. Clearly, I was chipped.

DID I JUST FLUSH MY BABY DOWN THE TOILET?

A few months went by, and I was pregnant again. This time I was ecstatic. Surely God wouldn't allow me to endure another loss. I was so sure this time would have a happy ending that I downloaded one of those apps that tracked my baby's growth every day. Speaking of daily growth, it felt like I was getting bigger every day. Everyone was excited. My husband, my mom, and our pastor freely shared our good news. Work was more stressful than usual, so my husband and I went on vacation the moment my schedule relented to be sure I was well rested, and our baby was safe.

The last night of our vacation, I began to spot again. "No, no, no, no, no. Please, Jesus, no!" We called the doctor first thing in the morning, and since my ultrasound appointment was scheduled for the following day, they told us they would take us as soon as we got there. We traveled from Pennsylvania to Ohio, then early the next morning we drove to the doctor's office. While waiting, my flow turned slightly pink, but I held steadfast to my faith. The nurse took us to the examination room, and I got undressed. She prepped me for and began the vaginal ultrasound. I anxiously looked at the monitor, and for the first time, I saw my baby. So tiny, like a gummy bear. I tried to relay the image of my baby on the screen with what my app said about his growth for that day, but the look on the nurse's face assured me it wasn't time to celebrate. "I'm so sorry, it looks like you lost him approximately two weeks ago," she said.

I immediately looked away and began to sob and scream without making a sound. My husband and I decided to wait until the doctor was available for me to be re-examined. We were met with the same disappointing news and a decision to make: schedule a DNC or wait until my body dispelled my baby on its own. After hearing it could take up to four weeks to naturally miscarry the baby, we scheduled the DNC for two days later.

As we drove home (40 minutes away), I felt excruciating pain in my back, so we stopped at Rite Aid to get maxi pads, just in case. While inside, I stopped in the bathroom. I didn't want to push, but I couldn't stop myself. I was in so much pain. As I miscarried in the toilet, I heard a loud thud, then the pressure subsided. Without thinking, I jumped up, turned to face the toilet and thought, *Just reach in there and get your baby . . . what kind of mother would flush her child down the toilet?* I extended my open hand toward what I imagined could have been my baby in the bottom of that toilet; as my fingertips reached the murky water, I blurted out, "*Bleep*, is you crazy?"

I CAME ALL THIS WAY FOR YOU

I had come close to losing my mind. I cleaned myself and the bathroom, put on a maxi pad, and walked out of Rite Aid. My husband asked if I was okay. "No," I whispered. He gently helped me into the car, and we continued to drive home. "Did I flush my baby down the toilet?" I screamed over and over again. Michael tried to console me, but I refused to be consoled. Then suddenly I had a brilliant idea . . . I wanted frozen yogurt. Clearly, I wasn't in my right mind; however, my husband tried his best to help me through this experience. He held my hand and drove me to get frozen yogurt. When we finally pulled into our driveway, my husband noticed there was blood all over my sweatpants. Once we were in the house, he called the doctor. While my husband was being instructed to take me to the hospital (40 minutes away back in the direction we'd come from), I continued to miscarry in our bathroom. I cleaned myself, put on a fresh jogging suit and some perfume, then Michael drove 110 mph to the hospital.

My mother, uncle, and cousin met us there. By the time they got to the hospital, I was in complete control—despite the fact I was still miscarrying. There were no more tears, no more screaming, no more craziness. I helped the doctors as much as I could. I stayed alert and informed them of any changes in my body temperature, when I experienced contractions, and whenever I felt like I was going to faint. Obviously, I was an integral part of my medical team (in my mind).

Once the team of doctors was done with the procedure and left the room, my husband carefully cleaned me up. The attending nurse said, "You don't have to do that, sir. That's my job." Then, she asked my family and my husband to step out of the room, to which Michael responded, "Ma'am, this is my job. If I can enjoy it when it's well, I can take care of it when it's in this condition." I almost passed out from embarrassment. Did he just say that, Jesus? "I'll clean her up; you can step out," he continued as he carefully washed me and gently reminded me how wonderful I was and how much he loved me. I never felt more vulnerable and exposed in my life, yet my feelings were mixed with an overwhelming sense of "That's *my* man!"

After a while, the nurse returned and I could tell she needed something, so I asked if I could pray with her. She said yes but wasn't sure if it would help. She kept saying she wasn't going to be around for long. At that moment, it all made sense. I said aloud, "I came all this way for you. If you would allow me to, I would like to pray with you."

The Pain Is Necessary

After a few days off from work, I slowly gained my momentum. Several weeks later, my husband and I went in for my follow-up ultrasound. The doctor explained the ultrasound showed several cysts—three small masses in my uterus and one large cyst embedded in the muscle behind my uterus. He recommended surgery. I refused to look at the monitor, and I honestly don't remember anything the doctor said after that. I did remember my husband asking him if he trusted the surgeon I was being referred to, and thinking, "I'm so tired."

The day of the surgery, my house was a mess. Piles of clothes were everywhere. Dirty dishes were in the

PAIN IS A NECESSARY PART OF THE HEALING PROCESS

sink. Dust was on the floors. Our unpaid bills were also added to the list of things to be taken care of. (We had the funds, but I didn't have time to pay the bills.) I did, however, make time to get a pedicure and a manicure. Clearly, I had my priorities straight.

That night, following the surgery, I let out a loud sneeze that echoed from my core to the rest of my body and caused excruciating pain. I don't know if the alarms I heard immediately after were real or a figment of my drug-induced imagination. The next morning, the nurse apologized that no one told me to hold a pillow to my stomach before coughing or sneezing. Then she said the most ridiculous thing I had heard at that time. "Mrs. Harris, you have to get up and walk now." I told her she was mistaken and that I'd just had surgery the morning before. I also reminded her that I almost sneezed my uterus out of my nose the previous night. There was no way I was going to get out of that bed.

While explaining how fearful I was of walking and how much pain I was in, the nurse comforted me with the most truthful, inspiring words. "It is going to hurt, but the pain is a necessary part of the healing process." I said, "Suga, can you say that again . . . the part about the necessary pain?" "Oh yes," she said. "It is going to hurt, but you have to get up and get moving, so you don't get stiff or get used to being stagnant. It's painful, but it's necessary if you're going to heal properly. We want you to walk the hallway twice today." With my head hung low, I thought about my four beautiful children whom I'd never seen. The tears swiftly rolled down my face as I pushed my legs over the side of the bed, planted both feet firmly on the floor beneath me, and slowly lifted myself up. Then, I walked. Not once, not twice, but five times that day.

I spent seven weeks at home, healing, resting, and walking around the couch in my living room. I was exhausted. My experiences left me completely drained physically, emotionally, and spiritually. I could tell my body was at "dis-ease" with how I had handled her and how I'd managed (ignored) stress over the years. Seven weeks is a long time to spend with yourself. I took inventory during that time and came to a few conclusions:

- I was a workaholic; I did not safely put myself first and consistently take care of me.

- I had a lot more work to do to establish and nurture a healthy rhythm that is effective for me.

- I gained weight because I ate too much, I was stressed, and I didn't exercise regularly.

- I had not spent significant time with my family and friends because I hadn't made time for them.

- I could no longer effectively juggle everything on my plate.

- I did not pray and spend quiet time with God like I used to.

- Stress may have caused many of my physical ailments, and if I didn't make a change, I would stress myself to death.

- If I died, my job and my church would move on without me.

- If I didn't make a change, I would waste the abundant life Jesus promised me.

I often thought about what my nurse said to me, ". . . pain is a necessary part of the healing process. You have to get up and get moving." My pain was evident, and my disappointment was real, but I needed to move forward. I decided to work again on the book you are currently reading. I prayed. I cried. I cussed. I wrote. More importantly, I embraced the pain and slowly began to heal.

UNPACK

By the end of the seventh week, I was stronger. I also knew my journey wasn't over. I returned to work, church, and life with a new resolve and added a new word to my vocabulary . . . NO! I said no to consistently working late. I said no to playing office politics and getting emotionally worked up when others didn't play fair. I said no to giving up all my free time every weekend to church activities or work. I said no to people calling me at any hour of the day and night to discuss their problems. I said no to my food addictions and that unwarranted, unsubstantiated feeling that my worth was tied to the thrill of ALWAYS being busy.

PACK

I said yes to quality time with friends and family. I said yes to monthly massages. I said yes to updating and reviewing our family budget on a regular basis and establishing autopay for as many bills as possible. I said yes *again* to daily quiet time with God, and yes to exercising, eating healthier, and actually going to the doctor instead of googling my symptoms. I said yes to monthly pamper sessions to get my polish together. I finally said yes to me!

Maintain and Nurture My Polish

Since that season in life, I have fallen off the wagon on numerous occasions. In fact, I must actively guard against giving work, home, and church 100% of me all of the time. Nowadays, I fall off the wagon less often, and when I do, I am quick to get my polish together.

Honesty is the key to my maintenance plan. I have to be honest about how I am feeling and how well I think I can effectively juggle all of my responsibilities. I try to start every day with prayer and quiet time with God, along with deep breathing and meditation on scriptures to settle my spirit and focus my vision for the day. Afterwards, I transition to my physical woman by working out. (My goal is a minimum of 30 minutes.) Then, I'm ready to face the day victoriously. I selflessly pamper myself on a regular basis and reassess the value of my relationships to ensure I create the most positive, affirming environment possible. Above all, I keep moving forward despite the pain that comes with this journey.

Seven Polished Questions:

1. **What advice would you give other women in a similar situation?**

   Put God first, take care of you, then put everything else into its proper place. Perfectionism is a disease that causes undue stress. It threatens your health and can only be cured by setting boundaries, accepting limitations, and boldly facing reality.

2. **Knowing what you know now, what would you tell yourself at the start of this journey?**

   Keep your eyes on Jesus. Life will present many distractions but stay focused. Take time to rest; you cannot keep running at this pace.

3. **What is your favorite beauty secret?**

   I put Vaseline on my eyes and lips every night.

   I create and use my own homemade pampering products as well: salt soaks for my feet, brown sugar scrubs for my feet, lips, and hands, and body butters for my body, baby!

4. **What is your favorite pampering secret?**

   Enjoy every moment of the day; it was made just for you. Laugh as loud, hard, and often as you can. Oh yea, take long, hot baths.

5. **As a woman, what is the best advice you have ever received?**

   "One moment or one event does not define who you are or who you will become, so get yo' *bleep* together!" Since I no longer cuss (I don't), I changed the last part of the statement to ". . . get yo' polish together!"

6. **Are you polished right now?**

   Yes, and my toes are polished because I recently got back on the wagon. But before this mental clarity, my toes and my life had transitioned from layered to chipped to darn near wrecked.

7. **Is a woman's sanity directly linked to her pedicure? Why or why not?**

Yes, especially if we're defining sanity by her ability to handle all her responsibilities—and the subsequent stress—while juggling everything on her plate, yet purposefully pampering herself.

Rebecca

FINANCIAL CHAMPION

When I moved away from home, I thought I could handle being on my own. I assumed finding an apartment, paying utility bills, and buying a car and furniture would not only be exciting but relatively simple. I had no idea this process of balancing my finances would be tougher than a $2.00 steak. At the time, I was a layered woman. I looked great, felt great, opened my own dance studio, volunteered at a program for at-risk kids, and traveled with a performance team. I even worked part-time as a Human Resource Generalist for a mid-size tech company. I was a college student living my dreams.

During this time, I accumulated a lot of debt. Managing finances with a demanding new life and a slightly out-of-my-budget apartment was very challenging (I opted for safety and convenience which cost a bit more than other apartments). Late fees, collections, threatening phone calls and letters . . . I got a real dose of reality shortly after living on my own. My finances were so jacked up that there were times I couldn't even afford simple necessities like tampons.

OFF COURSE

My parents taught me better. They taught me to save for a rainy day, to not spend outside of my means, and to budget. It was very difficult keeping up a life that appeared as though I was living what they taught me when I was really off-course. I knew I would figure it out once I focused on my finances, and if worse came to worse, I could call my parents for help. (Lord knows I wasn't looking forward to that conversation, so I figured it out.)

'Figuring it out' took some time. I remember traveling home after a dance performance across the country. I traveled by bus instead of plane, and my dad said, "Once you get yourself together, maybe you won't have to travel on the bus anymore." During that conversation, my mom also mentioned I'd received a few phone calls from creditors. I had to make a change. I was juggling my desired lifestyle and the reality of my finances with no experience and all the wrong tools. When a juggler can't maintain the timing, size, weights, and number of items in their juggling act, the performance is entirely out of sync. Eventually, everything comes crashing down around them.

I remember the day I realized I was a poor juggler. I came home, and my lights wouldn't cut on. I flipped the switch several times to be sure, but the electricity was shut off. So, I created a quaint, romantic ambiance with candles, and the next day, I paid my electricity bill. I also decided that there was no reason I should've been living that way. It wasn't that I didn't make enough money to handle my finances, I simply wasn't applying practical money management skills to my life.

My finances were out of sync. The more I tried to manage them, the more out of control they became. The first step I took toward financial wellbeing was planning to pay my creditors. I called to negotiate payoffs and tried to remain calm when companies threatened to garnish my wages, take my income tax money, or ruin my credit. I learned very quickly that cash is king. The more money I had to negotiate with, the more the creditors were willing to listen. I chose to utilize a temp agency for all my work, so my finances couldn't be tracked by the government for garnishment because they wouldn't know where I was working. I also stopped filing taxes for a few years. (I understand now that this behavior was inappropriate and completely out of control. Please don't judge me.)

Establishing credit and increasing my income was a slower process than molasses running uphill in the winter. I was faced with many choices in order to maintain my polish, one being to spend more money on professional clothing or find a job that required a uniform. I had to figure out how to continue to look polished and how to keep up with my hair, nails, fragrances, jewelry, body butters, lotions, treatments, creams, massages, etc. I was a fitness buff at the time, so to relieve stress, I would run a few miles outside, then I'd run the steps in my building. To pamper myself, I would take a one or two-hour dance class, then continue to dance when I returned home for a few more hours. The Bose speakers vibrated the walls and me. It was heaven. Jazz. Hip hop. Ballet. Modern dance. It didn't matter what class; I was grateful for the opportunity to stretch my body and release my mind to a creative space.

This did not fix my finances, but it did allow me to escape reality for a little bit. I operated as a pretty natural woman. Clear polish on my nails and toes and light makeup, if any at all. I loved my fresh and free look, and I never had to worry that I couldn't maintain it. I also lived very modestly, and to compliment my style, the look of my home was that of a minimalist. You know, only having what was needed and functional. There were very few decorative items or bulky furniture pieces. From the outside, it would appear I was conserving money and managing it well. I started to have available cash to participate in various activities. Spring break in Florida? Not a problem. Last minute weekend trip to Las Vegas? Of course. Club tonight? Uhm, yes. These luxuries would lead you to believe my lifestyle and polished look were my choice and not the result of the financial crises in which I found myself. You see, I juggled many things, including the perception of it all. Baby, I looked good, even if I dined by candlelight every night.

FOLLOW THE PLAN . . . RINSE . . . REPEAT

I was inspired to make more sustainable, long-term changes when one of my family members became ill, and I struggled to gain the finances to travel back home. This misfortune had a huge impact on me. I realized life is more than living in the moment. I began to understand the various meanings of the quality of life. The most important thing was to understand what it meant to me. I realized I have a responsibility to myself, my family, and my children's children to build wealth that can be passed down.

Just as I was wrapping my mind around my financial situation, another family member fell ill. I traveled home again. Then, reality set in. *Who will take care of my parents? Am I financially set up to support them? If my family or friends need anything, am I in position to help? Is my life solely centered around me and my desires?* I concluded I didn't have enough money to help anyone but myself. All of the unplanned events I was unable to attend was because my money was not being appropriately managed. I missed out-of-state weddings, trips with friends to exotic destinations, and other family and friend celebrations. I couldn't travel. I was grounded (literally). I knew I could have a better life that included unlimited world travel without financial setbacks.

I learned more about financial stability and became a huge believer in financial literacy. I spent days at half-priced bookstores researching and gathering books about becoming debt free. I watched television programs and attended free conferences on building wealth and eliminating debt. The most important thing I learned about money is I must control it. I learned what percentage of my income should be spent on living expenses (e.g., mortgage, car note, etc.). I also learned what I could afford based on my income and that good debt is when I use my credit cards to generate more revenue versus buying material items.

The next step in my financial security was to align myself with peers who were successfully driving their financial futures. I took money management courses then started working with an investment advisor. He evaluated the options I had to create a portfolio that would include minimal risk and helped me build my total savings while I cleaned up my outstanding bills. The investment advisor also helped me understand my earning trends, the possibility of multiple streams of income, and the importance of financial competency. My advisor taught me there is no need to learn everything about investing at first, but there is a need to start. Make moves with minimal risk. That way, you'll learn about what you're interested in so you can become an expert in that industry. Then, you'll know the trends and be better equipped to make financial decisions on investments with patience and intelligence.

My next epiphany was death . . . my own. My focus moved past the quality of life I have here on this earth to my family's financial freedom when I'm gone. Somewhere along my financial journey, I developed a desire to leave my loved ones with absolutely no debt once I transition. I also want to be able to assist others if needed. One day, I went to an economic empowerment summit and made friends with people who helped me become debt free and operate from the space of a lender instead of a borrower. To move forward, there were a few things I had to do to change my financial life:

- Accept the true economic status I was facing at that moment. The truth was, I was living above my means because I wanted a lifestyle that allowed for travel and safe, luxury living. My financial status was middle class, and I was living above that.

- Accept what I could and could not afford.

- Make a change or my cycle of bad financial behaviors would continue and possibly get worse. (Worst case scenario, I would have to confess my situation to my parents and maybe even ask for help.)

- Review and prioritize my outstanding balances.

- Develop a one-year aggressive plan to clear at least 40% of my debt and save or invest 10% of my income toward financial growth.

- Create a financial plan; break it down into weekly and daily goals to ensure success.

- FOLLOW THE PLAN. Establish some discipline.

- Set new financial goals as initial goals are met.

- RINSE AND REPEAT.

Naturally, I ran into many challenges while on my journey to financial wellness: travel opportunities, shopping deals and sales, car troubles, family needs, and broken appliances. I learned that anytime you set a plan in motion, you must expect the unexpected. I had to remember that we—people of God—were given dominion over the earth and the things in it. I had to remember that I can do all things through Christ who strengthens me. I had to change my mindset about money so that no roadblock could tempt nor deter me from my desired success. Prayer requires action, so I acted on my prayers and trusted my financial situation would turn around.

Unpack

Ultimately, I said no to bad choices. No one forced me to spend my money. I had to unpack a poor mentality of living in lack or with just enough. I said no to procrastination, poor planning, lack of financial knowledge, television, and other distractions that stole the quality time I had to effectively plan for my financial future. I said no to late fees, overdraft fees, additional credit cards, missed payment deadlines, and spending outside my means. I had to say no to all excess until I could get my finances under control.

Pack

I said yes to financial literacy. I said yes to understanding the industry of building wealth and yes to making better choices. Most importantly, I proceeded with action after I said yes.

There is a Bible scripture in the 23rd chapter of the book of Proverbs, and a wonderful book by James Allen titled, *As a Man Thinketh*, that I've read multiple times along my journey. I began to understand that my thoughts about money drove my decisions in how I used my money. I learned I must intentionally develop my financial plan because it doesn't happen on its own; there is no quick fix. I would either manage or mismanage my money well. It was my choice, and it all began with how and what I thought about my money; that's where my plan starts and ends.

Maintain and Nurture My Polish

I attended seminars and workshops, established friendships with people who shared their financial knowledge with me, and I acquired an investment advisor. I read and studied about finances, and I still have a plan to ensure I am growing wealth, as well as eliminating debt. I research based on the future. For instance, how much do I wish to have for retirement? What do I hope to leave for my children or grandchildren? How can I contribute to those in need? Once I began to understand my money is not all about me, my perspective changed. I am driven to create, develop, and seek more knowledge to maintain and increase opportunities for growth—not just for myself, but for others. Oh yeah, I still dance. I also still wear a natural-ish polish color on my toes and nails. I've upgraded to a natural pink color instead of clear BECAUSE I CAN AFFORD IT. LOL.

SEVEN POLISHED QUESTIONS:

1. **What advice would you give other women in a similar situation?**

   Utilize the internet and libraries to research how to regain control over your finances. If you like being involved with others, find a great financial guru to talk about your money. Develop a plan and stick to it. Remember, as you prove you are faithful over the lesser, you then will be trusted with the greater.

2. **Knowing what you know now, what would you tell yourself at the start of this journey?**

   Be patient but be more aggressive. You cannot talk yourself out of something you behaved yourself into. Less talk, more action. Believe that it will happen and trust that nothing can stop you. Remember there are two parts to the plan: grow wealth and eliminate debt.

3. **What is your favorite beauty secret?**

   My favorite beauty secret is dancing. Dance is wonderful for the mind and body. It unites cultures, generations, and is an excellent form of exercise. I dare you to try it for 30 days. Turn on some music, or go to a class or club, and dance at least three times a week for 2 hours each time. Then tell me what your legs, buns, skin, abs, and arms look like, and I'm sure you'll find the answer to why it's a beauty secret.

4. **What is your favorite pampering secret?**

   I pamper myself with a different form of dance: partner dancing. I go to a salsa or a stepping class to enjoy dancing with a partner. The room is usually full of people waiting to compliment you and willing to dance with you. In this atmosphere, the woman is adored. Much like on *Dancing with the Stars*, she looks beautiful and follows her partner's lead. Likewise, the partner is a gentleman, and the night is a wonderfully creative space to be swept away.

5. **As a woman, what is the best advice you have ever received?**

   The best advice I've ever received was to write my own personal mission statement (similar to what a company uses to share the values they abide by). I now have a personal mission statement and make daily choices that support the vision I have for myself.

6. **Are you polished right now?**

   I am currently in the space of transitioning into polished. I have to rinse and repeat my aggressive financial plan one more year before I will be polished and able to move to a standard financial plan, but I am claiming victory now.

7. **Is a woman's sanity directly linked to her pedicure? Why or why not?**

I do believe a woman's sanity is linked to how she pampers herself. For some, it may be a pedicure. For others, it may be dance. No matter the indulgence, it is critical to find time and space to rejuvenate, replenish, and breathe. Every woman deserves that.

MONIQUE
DENTAL ASSISTANT

My journey began at an early age because my aunt got a kick out of making fun of my "sugar cookie" feet, as she called them. She said that they were so ashy and in need of lotion that they looked like sugar cookies. As my aunt polished her toenails with bright red polish, she explained that ladies always keep their toenails polished. From that day forward, I realized pedicures were not only attractive, but mandatory.

Fortunately, that mandate transferred to my teenage and adult years. I learned my color preferences and spent countless hours soaking, buffing, filing, and meticulously polishing my sugar cookies. I had a few specific pedicure standards:

1. No chipping

2. Fingernails and toenails must match

3. NEVER wear sandals without being polished

POLISH . . . PAIN . . . AND POTENTIAL

While these grooming rules were ingrained in my mind, I never realized how much they were uniquely aligned with my natural and spiritual journey. You see, I believed people always needed to see me in a positive light. I wanted to look polished, even when I wasn't. I would best be described as the woman with multiple layers: polish, pain, and potential. I sincerely believed my pedicure (fresh or layered) caused others to hone in on my outward appearance. I assumed no one would challenge "my truth" because of it. My truth was I walked in such a magnanimous state of fear that everything I did was to either please people or prevent them from identifying my many insecurities. I allowed myself to remain in painful situations because fear kept me from directly confronting personal, professional, or relational issues. Instead, I found ways to evade the pain and/or discomfort by focusing on the superficial. Consequently, my adult life became filled with seasons of emotional and spiritual turmoil.

I vividly remember overhearing a phone conversation between my then fiancé (an older, well-established man in our local political arena who'd swept me off my feet) and another man. He said, "She's in the other room," (referring to me). As I listened closer, I heard an exchange that would mirror that of a man and woman. It was obvious that unusual compliments were being given because he said, "You're making me blush." Unfortunately, I was unable to speak at that moment. Fear gripped me because I was forced to face an uncomfortable, unspeakable truth: this man was not who I thought he was.

Although I gained the courage to ask why he gave that response, his answer was a series of circumlocutory thoughts. As a result, I spent years trying to deny what I knew was true . . . we were never going to get married. I didn't have the courage to walk away or confront similar awkward experiences throughout our relationship. I transitioned from being *layered* to completely *wrecked*. Depression hovered over my life for many years. The weight of this truth disconnected me from the internal joy I had grown accustomed to experiencing. It seemed utterly impossible to fight against the gloominess, sadness, and disparity that engulfed me every day. How could

I forgive? It became easier to justify dwelling in a place of bitterness and anger.

I moved from being happy with the man of my dreams to juggling a secret I would never share. Each day, I masked this silent pain by overcompensating in other areas. You see, because of the public position and reputation he held, I had to *be* a certain way. I tried to impress others with my humor, creativity, cooking, conversation, and political insight. Yet, my internal condition was tumultuous as I was afraid to release the truth to anyone. Unfortunately, it became evident that others were already aware of my pain and the impact it had on my outward appearance, which started to mirror how I felt inwardly. I wore dark clothing that was both dull and unflattering. This was a complete transition from being a sassy woman who enjoyed flaunting a unique, bright, and stylish look. The pain had paralyzed me both internally and externally. Fortunately, I had a core group of family members and friends who frequently deposited words of encouragement that kept me afloat. They all had an innate ability to highlight my strengths to help me maintain a measure of sanity.

MY TRUE SELF . . . ODD AND ECLECTIC

While God was trying to reveal my true self, I was busy holding on to an image of who I thought I should be. After spending numerous years in the shadow of others' opinions and conforming to what I had been told, it became increasingly difficult to imagine myself in any other way. How would I stand as a confident individual? I hadn't been taught to do that, and I wasn't sure how I'd be received by others if I didn't present myself in the way I thought others needed to perceive me. I wasn't even sure I knew myself well enough to stand against anyone who might challenge my authenticity. No one confirmed who I was and what I was created to do.

In some strange way, I wanted people to believe I was someone I wasn't. For example, many people believed I was a conservative woman, but the truth was (and is), I am extremely sassy. I would wear conservative clothing and speak in a "safe" manner; however, I love eclectic clothing and am most comfortable when I laugh out loud with my family and close friends. If fear hadn't had such a firm grip, the story about my fiancé would've had an entirely different outcome. Looking back, the awkward comments and unexplained situations would've resulted in angry (and possibly physical) exchanges. The combination of pain, embarrassment, and anger could've caused an extremely volatile reaction.

I gave the impression I was happy and forgiving. Yet, a vast portion of my pain was steeped in unforgiveness and bitterness, which led to depression. That wrecked season was the lowest season of my life. I sat down one long night and came to a few conclusions:

- Mentally, I had resorted to living outside of reality.

- Acknowledging the truth was too painful for my mind to embrace each day.

- If I didn't make a change, I wouldn't live very long because the pain was too great.

- If I did make a change, I was afraid of the shame associated with exposing this secret.

THE POWER OF PEOPLE'S OPINIONS BECAME LESS IMPORTANT

As I sought a deeper relationship with God, I began to see Him as my source. So, the power of people's opinions became less important. It became less important to look right and more important to allow Him to remove the layers of pain and fear. My sister's previous words of wisdom had come to pass. She had said I would know I was free when I didn't care what people said about me. When my fiancé verbally rebuked me for gaining weight and embarrassing him because I didn't respond appropriately to the other wives, girlfriends, and fiancés in our circle, I simply responded, "I don't care. And by the way, I'm leaving you!"

Now listen, I'm not crazy. I kept that ring. Since we weren't married, I wasn't entitled to anything else. After eight years, I left with my pride, my dignity, a newfound sense of worth, and that *bleeping* ring! I had to start again. Practically speaking, I had to rediscover the things that were important and unique to me. I had to rediscover my love for people, fun, and spontaneity. I learned to dive into creating things with my hands. It's how I express love. I'm sort of corny, and I like baking, crocheting, cooking from scratch, and designing unique gifts for birthdays, weddings, and showers. I love sitting in the audience of theatrical performances and getting lost in the storyline.

Most of this self-discovery came after being honest about what I did for other people and what I did to please God and myself. Asking myself why I was doing whatever I was doing became a routine exercise. Was it for accolades? Was it for approval? Or was I merely fulfilling a false obligation? Peeling away other people's opinions and endorsements was difficult but necessary. It was disheartening to acknowledge how much power other people possessed over me. But, when I found my voice, I realized my "No" meant no, and my "Yes" meant yes. Internally, it was still difficult to believe I was doing the right thing for myself. The power of manipulation had damaged my ability to make sound decisions and stand by them.

Eventually, that freedom enabled me to heal from the inside out. Remember, I was originally layered with polish, pain, and potential. After slowly admitting the truth about myself, my truth included my strengths and my shortcomings. Honestly, most people already knew what was underneath my *image* but admitting the truth allowed God's promise to manifest. He said we shall know the truth and the truth shall make us free. I had buried the pain associated with unforgiveness, deceit, and depression. Removing my false self-image allowed God to minister to that pain.

I learned to establish time alone with God to pray until pain no longer oozed from my pores. Whenever I felt the need to cry, I gave myself permission to do so as long and hard as I needed to feel relief. Worship became my place of escape as I learned to spend early mornings and late nights in my prayer room. Sometimes, I simply laid before God and allowed music to lift the depression, anger, and fear that would revisit me. Other times, I would confess my feelings to God. I told him how I hurt and asked him to lift the weight and help me to forgive. Frequently, those encounters involved intense, emotional outbursts that were both necessary and cleansing. I'd spent too many years in silence and needed to let go of what I'd tried so desperately to hide. I needed to trust God with the pain He never desired nor intended for me to carry.

Today, my true potential is being released. God has created opportunities for me to speak to women to help them regain strength after enduring painful situations. He uses my former experiences to serve as a platform for ministry. None of my pain was in vain. Victoriously overcoming pain inevitably equipped me to share that strength with others. What a beautiful cycle.

UNPACK

I gradually released the power of others' opinions and suggestions in my life. I stopped leaving room for people to deposit their views concerning me. I had to unpack my dependence upon others' perceptions of me, as well as my need for people's approval.

Additionally, I had to unpack my views of myself that were inconsistent with God's Word. Fear, doubt, unforgiveness, and depression had to be unpacked quickly.

Ultimately, I unpacked a fiancé who was more attracted to the image of a traditional power couple than living his truth.

PACK

This process was simplified because I sought a deeper relationship with God, and it became the key element in my journey to freedom. This walk involved daily prayer, quiet time in worship, and a new level of comfort with solitude.

More specifically, I released my attachment to phone conversations and social media and replaced it with inspirational books and worship CDs. I allowed worship songs to take me to a place of peace. Once I had internal peace, I was ready to *polish* the outside.

Plainly stated, I packed faith, self-confidence, forgiveness, joy, and peace. This was my formula for becoming polished without streaks.

MAINTAIN AND NURTURE MY POLISH

Naturally speaking, I've made a commitment to myself to receive professional pedicures on a monthly basis and hair appointments every two weeks. I have to continue to value the need for personal pampering. It forces me to allow a qualified professional to help destroy my natural tendency to *layer*.

Spiritually, I realize my pedicure is a representation of God's ability to do all things well. It's no longer my attempt to make it appear that way. Emotional polish is slightly different. I must remember to guard my conversations with family, friends, and co-workers. If I entertain the wrong conversations or involve myself in unhealthy interactions, I risk the possibility of emotional demise. Thus, I try to shift negative discussions, offer encouragement when people are low, and politely excuse myself from situations that threaten my peace.

SEVEN POLISHED QUESTIONS:

1. **What advice would you give other women in a similar situation?**

   If I could offer a word of advice, I'd have to say it's never profitable to be anyone except your authentic self. You see, it's essential to maintain the value of personal care (e.g., pedicures), but not to present a false reality. Most importantly, tell yourself the truth.

2. **Knowing what you know now, what would you tell yourself at the start of this journey?**

   God is going to show you the truth. Believe Him and follow His lead immediately.

3. **What is your favorite beauty secret?**

   I put olive oil on my lips to keep them soft.

4. **What is your favorite pampering secret?**

   On the night of my pedicure, I put Vaseline on my feet and sleep in socks. It helps my feet stay soft.

5. **As a woman, what is the best advice you have ever received?**

   Do everything with love.

6. **Are you polished right now?**

   No, not yet.

7. **Is a woman's sanity directly linked to her pedicure? Why or why not?**

   Yes. When we recognize the demands we place on our feet, it becomes important to pamper this essential part of our body. Neglecting our feet reflects the internal neglect that impacts our emotional, spiritual, and psychological well-being.

NICHOLE
EXECUTIVE ADMINISTRATIVE ASSISTANT

I met my husband in high school and thought he was the most handsome man that walked through the doors. Little did I know, he had been expelled from our rival school. I didn't get why he was expelled—and I had concerns about it—but we became friends the last two years of high school. I had a college boyfriend, so I wasn't interested in a relationship with him; besides, he had a trail of girls chasing after him (seriously, it was a hot mess). Little by little, we found ourselves exchanging notes in study hall. These notes were about our dreams and what we hoped to accomplish right out of high school. It intrigued me to see this man in this light. There he was, the most popular guy in school, and he was talking to me.

Valentine's Day came along, and my friend unexpectedly gave me a teddy bear and a card. He could have given this gift to any girl in the school, but he chose me. It was at this point I had to let him down easy because I figured I was too mature for him; besides, I was dating a man in college. It wasn't the greatest relationship, but my boyfriend was mature and already on the path to making things happen.

After high school, the most popular boy in school and I continued to run into each other over the years . . . at the mall, in restaurants, even at *Best Buy* as I was picking up a CD. It was fate, I guess you could say.

FIRST COMES MARRIAGE, THEN LIGHTS OUT

I always said that I wouldn't date anyone with kids; that was a huge NO in my book. Also, in this "book" of mine, I said my ideal man had to have nice shoes. I thought a man that took good care of his shoes meant that he could also take care of me, our home, and our children. I learned quickly that was not the case and got rid of my book. So, the most popular guy in school and I continued our friendship.

One day, he brought his son over to meet me (he had a son after high school). The moment I saw him interact with his child is when I noticed the change in him. He was more mature and grounded. He knew what he wanted and needed to do to make sure his son was in a stable environment. I could tell this by the way he looked at his son and made sure his schedule was always built around his child. I took a chance on my friend, and we dated for seven years. I accepted his son (who was a year old when I met him) as if he were my very own. He taught me patience and how my presence in his life was as important as his mother's and father's. Now don't get me wrong, his mother and I didn't have the best relationship, but I didn't let that scare me away.

In February of 2008, my boyfriend and I drove to our high school parking lot on our way to look at a home to purchase. I got out the car to check a sound coming from my engine; he followed behind me, and as I knelt, he kneeled with me. His next words were, "This is where it all started for us, isn't it?" I stopped and said, "What?" He smiled at me and repeated his half question. I was confused. "It sure was." He got on one knee and said, "Well, how about we start something new.

Will you marry me?" I fell back and cried in disbelief because he really caught me off guard. Not to mention, I was in my pajamas looking a mess. The nerve!

It has truly been a roller coaster of a ride, this marriage thing. When we returned from our honeymoon, things got real, real fast. They say the first five years of marriage is the hardest, and when we went through the process of planning the wedding, we laughed it off. See, here's the thing. When you live together, finances combine, bills come in, debts stack up, and the stress of job security rears its ugly head. I often think back on a particular incident when things got a little twisted. It was a month into our marriage, and I'd had the best day at work. My husband called me when I was almost home from work and said, "Don't be mad, but I have something to tell you." Red flag, right? He proceeded with caution and said, "The electricity is turned off." I was livid because he said he would take care of this bill. He didn't know you had to pay the bill in full or at least twenty percent to avoid having your electricity shut off. He was paying on it but not what he was supposed to. I took a moment to order my words and explained to him how the bill works and told him that he needed to let me take the lead when it came to paying our bills. This was an instance we needed to lean into each other. I had to lean in a bit farther because he was embarrassed, so we had that "We need to trust one another" conversation. The electricity has never been shut off again (nor any other utility for that matter), but it was in that moment my husband and I had to guide each other and work as a team. It would be the first test of many.

HE'S HERE, BUT WHY THE TEARS?

Time went on and we tried to have a child, but it was difficult. Then one day, it happened. I was pregnant (about three months to be exact). I had gone to the doctor appointments, heard the heartbeat, and thought everything was going well. Until one day, it wasn't. After a wonderful date night, I became ill and had to be rushed to the emergency room. There, they told us that I had miscarried. A miscarriage, how could that be? The heartbeat was strong . . . it must be a mistake.

My husband had to lean in a little further for me this time. He didn't understand what was to come in the aftermath of all this. He thought it would be fine because we could simply try again. But I didn't want to try again. I didn't want to go through this again. Besides, I had his son to give my affections to. His son's smile and laughter kept me from sinking into depression because he needed us to be present, regardless of what we were going through.

Six months after the miscarriage, I fell pregnant. Nothing was planned, we just went through with the process. I mentally prepared myself to keep positive and see what God allowed to be. It was a very difficult pregnancy and delivery (I almost died), but our son was born in April of 2011.

At one point during the delivery, the doctors asked my husband to leave the room while they gave me oxygen. I saw his love for me in his eyes. He didn't want to leave the room and demanded to stay. I wasn't sure what was going to happen, but I reassured him that it would be okay no matter what. As they ushered my husband out the door, I gave him a thumbs up and mouthed, "I love you."

My heart rate and my son's heart rate dropped fast. He wasn't getting enough oxygen. I was at peace, though. I knew that my son would be okay. God didn't bring me through every-thing for me to lose my child that way. Eventually, the baby and I were stable. The doctors allowed my husband back into the room, and I was instructed to start the pushing process.

When we brought our baby boy home, post-partum depression set in. Like marriage, I was forewarned about the challenges, but I thought I knew what I was doing and didn't need anyone's help. My first experience with the depression started when I sat in the rocking chair in my baby son's room and cried for no reason. At first, I blamed it on being happy that he was home and safe in our arms. However, the crying didn't stop.

When my husband went back to work, I found myself crying off and on, all day, for no rhyme or reason. That same day, I received flowers from my husband's job and when I answered the door to receive the delivery, I was a blubbering mess. I didn't know how to cope. When my husband came home on the fourth day of my maternity leave, I grabbed him around the waist as soon as he walked in the door and cried. I cried all the tears I thought I had in me. He thought someone had died. He was scared; I was scared. I had no clue what was happening to me. My husband started asking around and everyone told him it was the hormones, that it was normal, and they would calm down as my body healed.

Well thankfully, my bout with post-partum depression only lasted two weeks. But those were the longest two weeks of my life. I thought I was losing my mind, but my husband patiently and lovingly stood by me. I regained my composure and began to make preparations to return to work because I couldn't sit at home any longer. I had to feel like I was a part of something.

Finding My Rhythm

I became a working mom. I felt guilty leaving my son with my mother that first day. I had doubts about returning to work and leaving him, but I thought of the life I would be able to provide for him if I continued to work. I thought of events he would want to attend, toys he would want, and so on. Going back to work was a necessity. My mother helped by sending me photos of my son so I didn't miss things.

Within an hour or two on my first day at work, I was back in the game. I didn't miss a beat. I had to become the mother, the wife, and the administrative assistant all at the same time. I had a sense of empowerment and thought I could conquer anything that came my way. There was no time to be still. I had to be there for everyone at their beck and call, including the frequent doctor appointments because of my newborn.

There was one doctor appointment I couldn't make, so my husband stepped in while I stayed at work for meetings. I was sick to my stomach at the thought of my son getting three shots without me being present. I thought I was the only one who knew what questions needed to be asked. I thought my husband wouldn't know how to hold him the right way when he cried or was upset. But I leaned in and allowed my husband to grow into this full-time role. I realized over time he had missed a ton of things with his first child, and this was a new experience for him as well. He had to learn as I did.

This parenting thing is an around the clock gig. We had to be a team when it came to our son. I had this single mom mentality sometimes, and that simply was not the case. My husband reminded me to step back and let him lead when it came to appointments I couldn't make. He also realized I needed sleep some nights, and I am so thankful when I think back on it now.

My lunch breaks have become my only solitude, and I am grateful for that hour of peace. During my lunch breaks, I found myself thinking about how I was going to be there for everyone as well as myself. How were other women walking around with multiple children? I mean, they had to have a coping mechanism, right? I knew my son would be my only child; I would get scoffs whenever I would tell people this, but they don't know the shoes I've walked in. It was okay to feel like one child was enough. You can be comfortable enough in your own skin to know what you can mentally handle. I had things I still wanted to accomplish and having more than one child running around the house would put a strain on all of that. There are twenty-four hours in a day and there should be no reason that one of those hours isn't spent doing what I loved.

So, I made a list. I love to read, so I made it my business to make a list of books I wanted to read. I didn't have time to hold a book and read it page by page, so I went to the library every Saturday to get audio books. I would listen while I was at work for a little pick-me-up. I also love to get my hair done, so I made sure I had a standing appointment every other week. It was my recharge time, and it gave me something to look forward to during the long weeks. (The appointments are now every week; isn't that exciting?) I started getting a pedicure once a month in the spring and summer to make sure I was always sandal-ready.

HAPPY WIFE, HAPPY LIFE

Even in our uphill battles, our love remains unbroken and connected, as it was back in high school. We laugh. We cry. Well, I do most of the crying. I won't tell you my marriage is perfect because no marriage or relationship is. It takes a ton of work. But if you love each other and embrace the changes and obstacles together, nothing will keep you down. So, laugh and smile at each other, even when you have an argument. My husband makes me laugh even when I'm angry. I don't know how he does it, but he does. If one shines, we both shine. We embrace the struggles we face because it's what creates the strength and the bond we need for any future obstacles. We celebrate all accomplishments, regardless how big or small. So, am I happy? I'd say that I am. Am I polished? I'd say very much so. The overall experience and time it took to get here, I must say, was hard.

Unpack

I had to let go of what I envisioned the perfect mother, wife, and administrative assistant to be. I had to be the best version of myself. I let go of all the self-help books I'd clung to during my pregnancy. I let go of all the so-called TV show scenarios and movies about perfect marriages and careers. I no longer pack apologies for being me.

There will be times when you need a nap and you need to say, "Screw it, we're eating out!" There will also be times when you decline invitations to events because you're just plain tired.

Pack

I've packed some important details from some of the books I've read, like owning up to the need for occasional advice from others; speaking up and asking for help when needed; and knowing that no one is stronger or better than anyone else. There is no judgment when you are stepping into parenthood for the first time.

Maintain and Nurture My Polish

I am not afraid to lean in or simply say no. I have learned over time that the only person that stops you from doing (or maintaining) anything is you. I take the necessary steps every day to make sure I remember what is important.

You can't stress yourself out to the point you end up in the hospital. Half of the people you would almost kill yourself for will be the ones who won't even visit or send flowers while you are in hospital. That workload will be there when you return, so take the time necessary to make sure your needs are met.

SEVEN POLISHED QUESTIONS:

1. **What advice would you give to women in a similar situation?**

   Firstly, don't put limitations on yourself. You can do anything you want to do. When you take care of you, then you can take care of others. You cannot forget about you, especially when you are married with a family, juggling numerous tasks, and wearing many hats.

   Secondly, you must communicate with your husband. You must make sure you speak up when it comes to your needs. My husband knows I will tell anyone in a second if I am happy, sad, mad, or in-between. I tell him to give me a minute, and then I will reconnect after I get my bearings; this way, we don't have unnecessary outbursts. I can't stress enough to be sure you are talking about your feelings with your spouse. You must tap into each other's needs, wants, dreams, and goals. You can accomplish anything and build your dreams together. We are equals when it comes to this marriage thing, and we work hard at it every day to make sure we are in a good place.

2. **Knowing what you know now, what would you tell yourself at the start of this journey?**

   Do not fret, girlfriend! You must think great to be great. If you want to accomplish something, it can be done. You must take time to figure it out, so take the time. No one is going to judge you for taking a moment to figure out what you want to get out of this life we live. Only you know what you want and need. It is up to you to make sure you work at it daily, so you don't lose yourself while catering to everyone else's needs. Make sure you communicate that every day.

3. **What is your favorite beauty secret?**

I don't wear makeup at all, except for an occasional MAC lip gloss. But if I ever get the start of a red blotch or pimple, I apply a dab of Colgate plain white toothpaste before bed. When I wake up in the morning and wash my face, the redness will have gone, and the pimple will dry out. It's invigorating.

4. **What is your favorite pampering secret?**

My pampering secret is spending at least one hour a day doing something I love. It can be a TV show, a book, or even some social media time. The point is to do what makes me happy in that one hour. I enjoy a bit of silence every day. I have so much clarity after having that time of silence. Sometimes you find the answers and the truth you have been searching for when you are quiet. Don't let a hectic day get in the way of getting in touch with you.

5. **What is the best advice anyone has ever told you?**

The best advice I ever received was from my grandmother. She came to the United States from Panama and didn't know a bit of English. She taught herself the language, became a nurse's aide at the hospital, and then bought (and paid off) her home. In her words, "Nobody makes or breaks you. Only you can do that. Don't ever include the word *can't* in your vocabulary because it can be done." I try and make sure I live by those words daily.

6. **Are you polished right now?**

   Indeed! My polished manicure is always in need of a touch up here and there. Polish never lasts forever, just as life never deals you the same day. I make sure I have a standing appointment to keep my manicure in check. As in life, things change like the color of our polish.

7. **Is a woman's sanity directly linked to her pedicure? Why or why not?**

   We are excited and ready to relax when we go get our mani/pedi until the receptionist says, "Okay, please go pick out your color." Let's be honest, sometimes it takes us a minute to figure out what is going to work best for the next few weeks. We find ourselves staring at rows and rows of beautiful hues trying to pinpoint which one fits us. I can see that pedicure or manicure being linked to our mental space during that moment. It is all in the color that we choose.

Hey Suga,

I'm just checking in. You are more than halfway through the polished stories. Have you seen yourself or someone you know represented along the journeys these women have so selflessly shared? I'm sure you've been able to identify at least shadows of the various types of polished women. So, what's your opinion of the hypothesis so far? Do you think a woman's sanity is directly linked to her pedicure?

No matter what you believe, don't stop reading here. The remaining stories are as honest, encouraging, and thought-provoking as the ones on the previous pages. Keep reading—you'll be glad you did.

Always,

Patrice

KELLY

PHARMACEUTICAL EXECUTIVE

I t's hard for me to believe that it has already been 25 years (actually, a little more) since I made a concerted effort to work on me and my challenges with self-identity. It hasn't been easy, and I'm not always consistent. The woman I was some twenty years ago—or I should say the woman I was perceived to be—wasn't necessarily the woman I am today. Back then, I was a career-minded, single mother of paternal twins: a handsome, mild mannered son and a beautiful, fiery, rebellious daughter who reminds me a little too much of me.

Did you notice how I listed my career before my children? Well . . . that's only the start of it.

TWINS FOR CHRISTMAS

I loved and adored my children, but I was also selfish. (That's a difficult thing to admit.) In my world, there was this juggling act between being a great mom and working toward a great career. I've always been accused of putting my career before my family. I started working in retail at the age of 18. The hours were long and grueling. I decided to do whatever it took to be successful, and I figured if I put in long hours and worked hard, I would go far. But how much is too much? Let me tell you . . .

I was 24 years old and eight months pregnant with twins while seeking another promotion during the holiday season. Christmas time in retail can make or break a career, and I was hoping it would propel my career forward. This may sound crazy to most women, but I wasn't going to miss an opportunity to shine. I went into labor the night of December 3rd and delivered my beautiful twins the afternoon of December 4th. Guess what? I was angry! I was angry I wasn't at work, and I was angry my babies had come early and messed up my whole December. The birth of my children was supposed to be a moment I would never forget. Yet, all I could think about was work, more work, and how I could get back to work.

I rationalized my thoughts. *My kids would be there for the rest of my life and would never know I didn't stay home to care for them.* Besides, the month of December wasn't coming around again anytime soon, so I had to get back to work. I was so determined to get promoted and have a successful career, I returned to work on December 15th. Eleven days after having my babies, I went back to working 60–70 hours a week and wearing an industrial-strength girdle and some kind of science project for a bra. Thinking back on my decision, would I have stayed home with my newborns to capture precious moments? No. I wouldn't change a thing.

I'm not sure why I was so proud I went back to work eleven days after having twins, but I was. When my kids heard this story, I rationalized my decision by explaining I worked so hard for their benefit. I worked to provide them with the best possible life I could. I worked to show them that a woman could have a career and support herself and her children. I'm not sure if I really believed that at the time, however. Part of me worked for them and the other part of me worked for (and still is working for) me. It's that selfish. Putting my career opportunities first became second nature to me and, unfortunately, it became second nature to my kids as well. Let me pause here to acknowledge I never won any Mother of the Year awards. And if you're concerned that I didn't experience enough guilt over my decisions, let me assure you I experienced plenty of guilt.

I grew up with both parents—married 59 years—who did everything possible to provide for their children. My mother walked away from a potential career and got a job working nights as a waitress to ensure she was available to me and my siblings during the day. I'm fairly certain that's where some of my "mom guilt" came from. I felt guilty that I wasn't that mom—the kind of mom that would put her kids before her own desires, or marry and stay with the father of her children. Instead, I focused on what made me feel good about me. Not only did I feel guilty about not being the perfect mother, I also felt guilty about pampering myself because that was time I could have spent with my kids.

When my twins were babies, I went on a much-needed vacation with my girlfriends to Cancun, Mexico. Before I left for my trip, my grandmother felt it necessary to share her very critical opinion of my need to be pampered. She told me my children would forget who I was while I was gone. How dare she? Does a woman not deserve to take a break to be pampered? Do women from that generation truly believe they shouldn't feel pampered? As I tried to enjoy myself and feel the warmth of the Mexican sun on my skin, my mind was full of guilt. Thanks to my grandmother, my trip was ruined. I was terrified that when I came home my children would have no idea who their mother was. If I were a single father of two who went on a weekend getaway, would I have received the same criticism? Or would I have been told to enjoy myself because it was deserved?

SHE DOESN'T FALL FAR FROM THE TREE

My first wake-up call was handed to me through my beautiful, fiery, and rebellious daughter who was diagnosed with severe anxiety and OCD when she was six years old. After multiple second opinions, I took on my grandmother's advice that my daughter was seeking my attention and needed me to be available like she and my mother were for their children. So, I made a drastic change in my mothering style. I set out to be a good mom even if it killed me. I showed up to *every* dance competition, choir concert, softball and football game, cheerleading competition, and everything else I was required to attend. While at those functions, I wished I was somewhere else (like work) and hoped no one noticed my lack of interest and enthusiasm.

School choir concerts were the worst. (Now that I have a grandchild, they are still the worst.) It was almost impossible to find my own kids in the sea of children. They were all dressed the same with the same glossed-over expression on their faces. Mothers, please tell me you know exactly what I am talking about? I was usually the mom in the audience with a purse on my lap, so I could hide the light of my phone as I worked while my kids were singing on those wobbly risers. I would look up and smile occasionally, just in case my son or my daughter was looking for the admiration of their mom.

After the concert was over, I would tell them how impressed I was with their performance, but that daughter of mine wasn't dumb. She knew I was working, and of course, she shared her observations with her brother. I would've been devastated if anyone else knew I wasn't the mom I was pretending to be. I was already consumed with guilt knowing my children saw right through my intentions. Perception became more important to me than my reality. That's why I went to every event. That's why I carried the Louis Vuitton purses, drove the Mercedes, wore the Rolex, and bought things I couldn't afford. Perception, perception, perception. I thought I was doing all the right things. My career took off, and my son excelled in every sport imaginable.

As for my beautiful, fiery, rebellious daughter? Well, let's just say she kept me on my toes. My daughter is bright and loving, but she can be exhausting. Let me explain severe anxiety through two examples. My daughter was a late bloomer when it came to puberty, so during her fourteenth year of life, I had to schedule two separate doctor's appointments to solely help me explain basic anatomy. The first appointment at the beginning of the year was arranged because she saw a story on the news about breast cancer—and since she had lumps on her chest (a.k.a. her breasts were starting to develop)—she was convinced she had breast cancer. This revelation went on for months, and there was nothing I could do or say to convince her otherwise. She would show me how she was going to wear a scarf on her head to hide her hair loss that was coming in due time. Someone with severe anxiety does not rationalize, no matter how hard you try. After attempting to reason with her and screaming at her to stop being ridiculous, I took her to our pediatrician. As we walked out of the doctor's office after her appointment, my daughter said, "It was really silly for me to think I was dying of breast cancer. I'm only fourteen. Mom, why didn't you tell me I didn't have breast cancer?" *What? Was this kid serious?*

That's not even the best story.

By the end of that same year, my daughter still hadn't started her menstrual cycle. All her friends had, so in her mind, something was wrong. This time, she convinced herself she was pregnant. Yes, pregnant. Now, I know some girls are promiscuous early in life, but not my beautiful, fiery, rebellious daughter. She didn't even know what sex was, let alone like boys yet. (I would later find out she was never going to like boys.) Once again, I spent weeks trying to rationalize with her, only to end up in another screaming match about how ridiculous she sounded. One day, I got a phone call from my mother informing me my daughter was telling my mother's neighbors that she was pregnant. Of course, it was my mother's opinion that if I spent more time with my children, I wouldn't have this problem. This time around at the doctor's office, I finally gave into the recommendation of giving my daughter medication. But before the end of the visit, the pediatrician had to convince my daughter that she wasn't pregnant, and the medication wouldn't harm her fictional baby. *Exhausting.*

I fought a constant internal battle for years because I struggled with the idea of medicating my daughter. When she was diagnosed with severe anxiety, I was told multiple times that she needed medication to control her behavior. *What kind of mother would that make me?* Once she started the medication and was able to function like a normal teenager (if there is such a thing), I started to question myself again. *What kind of mother am I?* My daughter had been miserable, not because I was absent but because I didn't get her the help she needed. (I'd thought the medication would be proof I was a bad mom.)

She attended weekly sessions with two different therapists shortly after starting the medication. I recruited my family to help take my daughter to these appointments because I was focused on my career again, and I was afraid I would miss something if I wasn't at work. I was afraid I would be looked at as a mom who couldn't handle the pressure of raising her own kids, instead of the professional woman I so desperately wanted to be seen as. Soon, I was revisited by my old familiar friend: guilt.

In her late teens, my daughter was angry, upset, and sometimes, plain psycho. (Between the two of us, there was too much estrogen in one household.) My son would often threaten to call our Priest to perform an exorcism on the both of us. My beautiful, fiery, rebellious daughter would habitually remind me of every time I chose work over being a good mom. It's like she had a list under her bed to which she kept adding. We had a life-changing moment during one of our fighting-about-nothing episodes at the start of her senior year in high school. When my daughter began screaming her list of bad-mom decisions, she yelled, "I'm gay, but you've been too busy at work or pretending to be present to even notice." "What? You're gay?" *Have I really been that busy and missed all the signs? What are the friggin' signs? Have I been in denial? What was happening to my life and my children's lives? Are identity crises hereditary? Did I create this?*

In that moment I saw it all. I saw the torment and pain in my daughter's face, and I understood my son's over-drive to be perfect. It wasn't their successful mother who was causing the problem; it was their absent mother who'd created a void they were ill-equipped to fill. My beautiful, fiery, rebellious daughter refused to wear makeup, dress up, or comb her hair. She wanted to be nothing like me. Wow, that was a hard pill to swallow. Interestingly enough, my son dated every pushy, loud-mouthed, opinionated, overly confident, competitive, too-much-makeup and big-hair-wearing girl he could find. I hated every mini-me he introduced me to.

Where did I go wrong? That was rhetorical; I knew exactly where I went wrong. My quest to appear perfect and give everyone 100% of me caused me to neglect everyone.

I CAN SEE CLEARLY NOW

I realized that taking care of myself is as important as taking care of my family and my career. Working toward a clear, realistic vision for who I am and who I want to be must be a priority. I worked hard to rewire that part of me that only felt good when I successfully convinced everyone around me I was what they needed me to be. Eventually, I came to a few conclusions:

- My mental state was spiraling out of control.

- I wasn't sure what being a good mom looked like (but I was sure I wasn't doing it).

- I wasn't sure what a successful career woman looked like (but I knew the woman I had become wasn't the woman I wanted to be).

- I needed to make a change before my biggest fear occurred—my children would look back at their childhood and say they weren't happy. Then, all my hard work to give them what they needed and wanted would be for nothing.

Slowly, I crawled toward honesty and holistic health. As women, I think we're expected to do everything: establish a successful career, raise children to be responsible adults, keep the house clean, do the laundry, cook . . . and the list goes on. I fell into the trap of letting those listed items define who I was. Eventually I came to the realization that I wasn't only a mom, cook, maid, or career-minded professional. I developed a vision for myself. I wanted to have it all and be good (not perfect) at it all by spending more guilt-free time on myself. I deserved that.

I still attended many school functions, sports events, cheer competitions, and other activities I dreaded; however, I changed my focus. It was no longer about watching my kids pretend to sing. (Let's be honest, they were lip syncing and didn't want to be there either.) Instead, it became about the moments we were sharing. We turned those dreaded activities into experiences. We made time before events to get Starbucks or time after the games and performances to grab dinner. We celebrated our time together. Although I never, ever, ever enjoyed attending my kids' extracurricular events, I learned to look forward to the time I spent with them before and afterward.

Along with motherhood, I had to take a hard look at my finances, a.k.a. my Mercedes. Was the stress of paying my bills every month worth driving a Mercedes? Hell yes, it was . . . at least for a little while. Every time I got in that car, I felt good.

At some point, my feelings changed. Every month when I wrote the check for my car note, I could feel my shoulders tighten. My mind would race, and I would have sleepless nights wondering how I was going to pay all my bills the following month. Every month, I made minimum payments on my credit cards which I used for buying material things.

When my twins were seniors in high school, I remember thinking I wish I could trade all those material items for their college tuition. The months prior to my kids starting college were terrifying. I didn't have the financial evidence I needed to support why I chose work over them all those years. But then I thought, *"Heck, they're almost adults and are capable of working their way through school. Besides, hard work builds character."* Who was I fooling? Who was I trying to impress all those years? Were my purses really that impressive when I could've bought knockoffs that looked as good? (Those purses could have been a semester of college.)

It was time to trade my Mercedes in for something more practical. Ugh, the word *practical* made me feel old, but the stress of paying for a car that I couldn't afford was actually making me look old. The morning of the trade, I shed a few tears. (I know . . . ridiculous. It's only a car. I should've been happy to have a safe vehicle.) I said goodbye to my elite status. I'm not going to lie; it took me a couple of months to recover from the breakup. It was like I was ending a loving relationship. I was devastated, maybe even a little depressed over it. But as the saying goes, "Time heals *most* wounds." Then it happened: one night I fell asleep without worrying about being perfect, my finances, or the lists upon lists of bad decisions I've made.

UNPACK

Saying no is not an easy thing to do unless you want to keep your sanity. I had to say no to my unhealthy love affairs (i.e., my Mercedes, my perceived status, the guilt I felt when I didn't get things right). I had to say no to my twins when they wanted to go somewhere or do something that didn't fit in with our schedule. If I didn't say no, I would've ended up paying for it later with stress. I had to let go of some friendships that I couldn't manage any longer. If the relationship was more exhausting than joyful, I slowly disengaged.

PACK

I safely said yes to me. I said yes to twenty uninterrupted minutes every day to focus on my mental health, peace, and well-being.

MAINTAIN AND NURTURE MY POLISH

I started with twenty minutes a day. I called them "MY twenty minutes", and I still honor this daily ritual. I do whatever I want for me (and only me), and I rebelliously refuse to feel guilty about MY twenty minutes. Some days, I turn my music up loud and dance. A little Michael Jackson goes a long way for my spirit. "Annie, are you okay? Are you okay, Annie, are you okay?" This Annie is definitely okay as long as I have MY twenty minutes. I also walk three to four miles every day and spend time every week polishing my fingers and toes.

SEVEN POLISHED QUESTIONS:

1. **What advice would you give other women in a similar situation?**

   Don't allow others and material items to dictate who you are or who you want to be.

2. **Knowing what you know now, what would you tell yourself at the start of this journey?**

   I wish I would've known years ago that twenty minutes a day can change everything. MY twenty minutes show my daughter that everyone deserves moments to focus on themselves. It also shows her that you need to focus on yourself to be a better woman.

3. **What is your favorite beauty secret?**

   Scrub and lotion. In the shower, I scrub away the previous day and lotion on the new day and possibilities that await me.

4. **What is your favorite pampering secret?**

   A hot bath a couple of times a week. I lock the world away and focus on me. I daydream about the warm sunshine on my skin.

5. **As a woman, what is the best advice you have ever received?**

   My favorite successful woman recently gave me this advice, "Always run to your next opportunity; never run away from the unknown." It is now how I make any major decision.

6. **Are you polished right now?**

   Yes, I try to stay polished by giving myself twenty minutes a day. I keep a schedule of how I'm going to spend MY twenty minutes to keep myself stable. Sunday is for pedicures. Monday is for manicures. Tuesday belongs to the treadmill. Wednesday is date night with Michael Jackson, and so on. I stick to my schedule every week.

7. **Is a woman's sanity directly linked to her pedicure? Why or why not?**

Yes! A woman, by nature, is constantly running around taking care of others. When I look down at the feet that are carrying me, I want them to feel and look good. I thank God every day for these feet that get me from place to place. If my feet are not healthy, I am not mentally healthy.

WENDY

ENTREPRENEUR

Robert and I moved in together our junior year in college and got married four years later. Our relationship was based on mutual activities, sports, and good sex. It wasn't until the photo shoot of our engagement pictures I realized we had no emotional connection. On the last shot, the photographer instructed us to face each other and look into each other's eyes. As we gazed lovingly at each other, I thought, *Wow, I don't see him, and I don't believe he sees me.*

On the way home, I asked him what he saw when he looked at me. He described only physical attributes. When I told him, I don't think we actually see each other, it was like I was speaking a foreign language. He had no clue what I was talking about, so I talked it over with my friends. "You can't have it all. That man takes good care of you, you have fun together, and he is fine." Deep in my heart, I knew this emotional disconnect was going to be a problem, but I thought it would resolve itself over time. Fast forward 32 years; we are sitting on the deck of our home, having the most emotional conversation we have ever had. Our marriage had come to an end. He said he finally understood the emotional connectivity I spoke of all those years ago. He said he was able to really see his mistress, and she was able to see him.

INTO *ME* SEE

I thought I would start my story right there, then drop the mic. You can probably guess my polished type. I was wrecked. Let's be clear, I was wrecked way before that moment with my husband. Truth be told, that moment was the beginning of the journey to becoming the polished woman I am today. You already know the beginning of my marriage was based on my *hope* that I could create something that wasn't there. But let me give you a little bit more. Five years into our marriage, I was a stay-at-home mom with four kids, all less than two years apart in age. Besides being well-kept, I loved that we always had something to do. We shared common goals like health and fitness, sports, church, and the arts. To loved ones and neighbors, we were considered the golden couple with the perfect family. We were an upper middle-class family raising four beautiful children, but underneath it all, I was chipped. Behind closed doors, my marriage was disintegrating under the weight of emotional detachment and the lack of in-to-me-see (intimacy). Crumbling from my husband's indulgence of pornography, and later discovering that "porn would never turn into real people" was a promise too substantial for my husband to keep, we had a real problem. I publicly kept the façade going, but secretly I was dying inside.

My marital relationship became really stressful in year five when I found out my husband was addicted to pornography. I prayed, and it seemed God didn't hear nor respond to my distress. It seemed like my husband got nastier as time went on, and I became nice nasty. I still managed the home with a smile on my face to the rest of the world, but when it was just the family, my pain and anger came out sideways with snide, cutting remarks. I even withheld sex at times. This was bad because the very good sex we'd once had in abundance now made my skin crawl whenever my husband touched me. My once strong physical attraction to him began to make me sick. I felt like a prostitute because sex was nothing more than physical, and I couldn't wait to shower afterward. I regressed from a peaceful, joyful woman to a bitter, resentful woman (all with a smile on my face).

WARRIOR PRINCESS

I decided I wasn't going to lose my husband to some silicon-injected, fake-moaning-and-groaning-on-the-internet bimbos! Aside from triple Ds, what did they have that I didn't have? I became laser-focused on trying to please him. My husband would say I had to help him get over this problem, so I thought more sex would do it. I kept my body fit. I loved him more. I pulled out a few tricks I had up my sleeve that would get us on track. Robert worked out of town a lot, so every time he came home, I had a hot, new, and sexy wig. He loved it! I would call him and say, "There's a new girl in town waiting for you." He named the wigs and created a fantasy storyline for each one, and I would take on that desired character when I put *her* on. With my vast selection of sexy lingerie and several bags of wigs, I created full characters and romantic scenes for him to come home to. I always kept him guessing. He loved my free spirited, adventurous side, but after a while, I couldn't remember the names of the darn wigs and the characters I was supposed to be playing. *Was I the dirty farm girl with the Asian accent? Or the African Princess Warrior who spoke German?*

The characters and romantic scenes helped for a season, but Robert always returned to pornography. Initially, I accepted him blaming me because I was not bigger, fuller, better, or more. He would say it was my fault he was hooked on porn because I wasn't giving him enough sex. *What do you mean? I was three different women this week.* It took me a while to sort out what was my fault and what wasn't. To prove to myself and to him that I was not to blame, I gave him sex whenever and however he asked.

One day, I came home and felt something off-putting, so I asked if he had been watching porn. He replied, "Yes." I asked why that was necessary when we'd had such a wonderful sexual encounter that morning. He said I put it on him so good he had to go look at porn afterward. That's when I knew it wasn't my fault. It was *his* issue.

As time went on, I became emotionally involved with a man whose conversation I enjoyed. I tried to deactivate that part of me that is hard-wired for connectivity because I knew I wasn't going to get it from my marriage, but the depth of my being screamed for it. I can honestly say I never intentionally went looking to connect with someone else. I fought to not let it go further than talking. I refused to have sex with him, but I still felt guilty. After several years, I confessed my emotional affair to Robert. I remember telling my husband that I was attracted to this other man's conversation about world events, religion, sports, politics, and so on. My husband's reaction was very nonchalant. He simply said he would step it up, which he did for about a month. Then, he returned to his status quo and an internet vixen with whom I was never going to be able to compete.

I continued my emotional affair until my best friend came to my house one morning and forced me to go to a Bible study with her. I went to the Bible study, sat down with a major attitude, and wondered what I could possibly gain from the group of old ladies. They were studying the book of Revelations and by the end of class, I was ready to repent. The lesson was about the church of Ephesus leaving their first love, and it impacted me greatly. I repented, ended my emotional relationship with the other man, and returned to God . . . my first love.

The final straw came when Robert confessed that he'd had a one-night stand two years earlier. As he laid out the details of his indiscretion, it all lined up. He had been out of town for the weekend, and when he came home, we'd immediately had sex. I remember stopping mid-way to ask him, "Are we okay? Something seems off." He looked me in my eyes and declared that all was well. All was not well. He'd had sex with another woman the night before, then came home and had sex with me. "I'm sorry, I'm sorry!"

I felt something break deep within me when he uttered those words. Although I was diagnosed with stage 4 breast cancer a few years later, I believe that was the very moment cancer entered my body. (I've read studies that show some forms of breast cancer may be linked to emotional trauma or stress.) Robert tried to win me back by being more affectionate. "Why are you trying to connect with me now after devastating me with such news?" I would ask. I refused all his efforts because I didn't want him to get off that easy.

Paralyzed with every negative emotion you can imagine, I was walking death. Well, not too dead because I went ahead and had my own affair; a real affair this time, not only some emotional support and intriguing conversation. The intense, prolonged, and unspoken pain I experienced lured me into the arms of another man who saw the real me the second we met. This time, I went over the edge and I didn't care. I didn't care what God or anyone else said. I threw caution to the wind and completely allowed my mind and body to embrace all of him. I shut my convictions down, and I stopped reading my Bible. I finally had the emotional connection and the physical satisfaction I'd always fantasized about.

I broke all my own rules with this man. I had an insatiable appetite for his presence. How can I describe it? How can I justify my behavior? It was like I was waking up after years of being asleep. It was like charging a dead battery when we connected; I felt completely alive. So much so that when my gynecologist examined me, she said, "Oh my, something has changed." The doctor said my va-jay-jay had had a failure to thrive look previously, so she knew something was going on.

I couldn't get dressed and out of there fast enough. At first, I couldn't stop smiling, then I couldn't stop crying.

ENOUGH

The thought of God looking down at me in this man's bed and envisioning how heartbroken He was at this scene is what eventually moved me past this season of weakness. I knew God was wooing me back to Him. It did, however, take a few more times of being in that bed. One day, my lover asked if I was ever going to leave my husband, but I couldn't outwardly defame the name of God and myself by making such a bold move even though I was secretly doing it. Eventually, he moved on. As time progressed, we found ourselves touching base with a conversation or text, but we were never physically or emotionally intimate again. To hold me accountable, I asked a group of prayer warriors to cry out to the Lord on my behalf. They prayed intensely for me, encouraged me with God's Word, and rebuked my sinful desires all while lovingly embracing me. Their love and tenacity were essential in overcoming delays, roadblocks, and potholes.

Let's go back to where I started this story.

There we were, Robert and I, sitting on our deck and weeping the loss of something we'd never really had a hold of. I had just told him about my diagnosis with stage 4 breast cancer and that I needed his emotional support through this. In return he said, "I love her, and I want to be the kind of husband I know I can be to her." I was devastated by his words. I thought about all my effort and how I revealed my heart to him. I thought about how I encouraged and supported him throughout the years . . . and this other woman gets to reap the benefits? I was hurt, my mind quickly reflecting on the number of times I had asked the same question in various ways: how can we address our lack of emotional connection, and what can we do to fix it? In the last six to ten years before our divorce, Robert stopped trying to change. He simply slapped that visa card down on the table and said, "This is as good as it gets. I'll buy you the world and treat you like the queen of England, but you're not getting what you want emotionally." He simply couldn't do it . . . not with me at least.

Yes, I wanted to drive him to the desert and put a bullet in his head. Yes, images of him floating at the bottom of the Atlantic Ocean danced through my mind. But when those thoughts came, reality set in. We had done enough damage to each other already.

UNPACK

I decided to surrender my total being to God. I began to seek His will and do things His way. I unpacked my own will and said no to the most intense longing for another human being I had experienced. I said no to an illicit relationship that completely satisfied me on levels I didn't know existed. I said no to blaming my ex, but ultimately, I had to say no to my marriage.

PACK

To move forward, I packed a new surrendered will. I packed a new commitment to return to my first love, God. I packed my Bible, a new listening ear and heart of obedience, and a new church. I also physically packed what I could into a moving van, and I moved out of my house. Interestingly enough, the hardest thing to pack was my real truth. I wandered away from God and my marriage when things didn't go the way I thought they should. It took me a while to own this truth but doing so allowed me to embrace another life-changing fact: God loves me, and I'm going to survive. What else did I pack?

1. Christian counseling and a Divorce Care class at my new church.

2. New friends who spoke life into me, encouraged me, and prayed for me.

MAINTAIN AND NURTURE MY POLISH

Over time, large doses of God's Word began to transform my mind, which directly impacted my choices and emotional state. I devoured the pages of my Bible. Of course, my flesh fought against it by suddenly getting extremely tired as soon as I opened my Bible (but once I closed my Bible, I was energetic). Nevertheless, I read my Bible anyway. During my prayer time, the intimate moments with my former lover would flash through my mind; my loins would yearn for him (I just knew I was going to hell). But I would combat those thoughts with repentance by saying, "Here, Lord, take this thought from me. I lay it under the blood. Wash me clean." I begged the Lord to stop my body from yearning for my former lover. The Lord didn't answer that prayer, but I learned to tell my body, "No, you can't have him anymore."

The more time I spent with God, the more He spoke directly to me from His Word. I'll give you an example. During one of the most profound moments with God, I was lying in my bed, paralyzed with the pain of all I was losing. I was balled up in the fetal position, then God said to my spirit, "Let go and feel the pain. I am with you in it." I replied, "No, Lord. This pain will kill me if I feel it completely." God kept saying, "I am with you in it." I let go and felt the most excruciating pain throughout my entire being. At the height of the pain, I felt a comforting weight on me, and the pain was now hitting the buffered weight around me. Although I felt it, I couldn't feel the piercing intensity of it. I stood at my bedside, put my hands on my hips like Superwoman and declared, "I can take anything now because I just came through the fire of pain. I'm ready for whatever, Lord."

_____
I SAW HIS HURT AND CAME
TO THE REALIZATION THAT
WE'D HURT EACH OTHER
_____

I began to see my ex-husband differently. I no longer looked at him as someone who deliberately hurt me. I saw his hurt and came to the realization that we'd hurt each other. On another occasion, the Lord said a healing balm for me would be to treat my ex with kindness. I obeyed the Lord and have been reaping the benefits ever since. My love for God has deepened and surpassed the pain of my past.

SEVEN POLISHED QUESTIONS:

1. **What advice would you give other women in a similar situation?**

   Do not satisfy your pain with sinful choices but run toward God in your brokenness instead. Reach out to prayer warriors—women with strong faith who are not afraid to say the hard things to you—to hold you up. Consistently attend a good church where the Word of God is preached with love and compassion. Keep it real with yourself and with God. Stand in your own truth no matter how ugly and painful it is. Know that God still loves you as you stand in your mess, and He is coming to rescue you.

2. **Knowing what you know now, what would you tell yourself at the start of this journey?**

   Keep your panties on! Believe God's Word no matter what it looks like. I spiraled out of control when I thought God didn't hear my cry for help. When I got to the other side, I asked God why He didn't answer my prayer to heal my husband. God said, "I heard your cry, and I answered. I sent Robert many ways of escape, but he chose not to take them, making it look as though I didn't hear or answer your cry." God hears you even if there is no change.

3. **What is your favorite beauty secret?**

My favorite non-tangible beauty treatment is resting in God's peace. This keeps the body from being severely attacked by stress. I learned this on the other side of my journey.

My favorite tangible beauty treatment is a good sugar scrub. There's nothing like well-polished skin.

4. **What is your favorite pampering secret?**

The women in my family taught me how to hit pause and pamper myself. Every Wednesday when the kids took a nap in the middle of the day, I would take a bubble bath while listening to soft jazz and sipping Kool-Aid or apple juice in a wine glass. Now, I retreat to a candlelit shower with my favorite worship music, shower oil, and shea butter sugar scrub. I complete the routine with one of my favorite body moisturizers. This pampered process always makes me feel beautiful, relaxed, and loved.

5. **As a woman, what is the best advice you have ever received?**

My auntie said, "Mankind is subject to error, therefore, reserve a little of yourself for yourself. Don't give a man all of who you are." She said she married her soulmate of 37 years but still held back a little of herself in case he decided to flip a switch, so she wouldn't lose her sanity because she'd given up all of who she was. Plus, she said, it creates enough mystery that will keep him intrigued while wondering and discovering new things about you.

6. **Are you polished right now?**

I have on a base coat and a good first layer of polish. My second and topcoats must be applied.

7. **Is a woman's sanity directly linked to her pedicure? Why or why not?**

A woman's sanity is directly linked to her pedicure because when her life is balanced and her stress levels are low, she has room in her mind to think about giving attention to her feet. She is in touch with her value and has no problem saying, "I deserve a manicure, pedicure, a massage, or whatever else makes me feel pampered."

DEBRA
EVENT COORDINATOR

"You have diabetes." Those three words affected me more than hearing the words "You're pregnant" at 19 years old. I'm not sure what would have been worse: being told I was pregnant again, or that I'd been diagnosed with diabetes. Let me backtrack and bring you up to date.

In 2010, I retired from the United States Navy after 20 wonderful years of service. I joined the military straight out of high school and never looked back. While active in the military, I maintained a somewhat healthy lifestyle. I worked out and learned about healthy eating. To be honest, I never applied the knowledge of healthy eating; I merely learned how to outrun a bad diet. I joined the U.S. Navy weighing 118 pounds, and I maintained a small frame until I hit my 30s. My *thickness threshold* slowly increased. At first, I loved it because I was thicker in areas that were attractive . . . until back fat appeared. My travels in the Navy required me to live in a new place every three to four years, so as I gradually put on more weight, I knew I would eventually move to a new state with new people who never knew the skinnier me.

I was accustomed to being thin. The day I delivered my baby I weighed 126 pounds, and three days later I was back to 100 pounds. I rested on the fact I was skinny and could eat anything without gaining weight. However, like most women, something happened to my body during the third decade of my life. After thirty, the female body is less forgiving; it slows down physiologically. Hormonal imbalances start to increase, metabolism starts to slow down, and so on.

It wasn't all bad, though. I was excited when my breasts miraculously started growing. But then my doctor told me it was fat, and I needed to lose some weight. I'd never heard those words before that day. My grandmother, mother, aunts, and whole family had always tried to fatten me up. Now this *heffa* (I was emotional so that was the name the esteemed physician was given) was telling me I was fat. She went on to talk about body mass index, waist circumference, and blah, blah, blah. I left her office and said I would show her.

Losing weight wasn't easy. I had adopted poor eating habits. I ate what I wanted, when I wanted, and portions over and above what I needed. These habits were hard to break. My weight, ironically, never affected my military service. I still ran like Flo Jo or Florida Evans (I'm not sure which one). Hell, I was even the fitness leader for my unit and taught aerobics classes.

I finally reached the point where I was tired of the whole weight issue. That moment came in 2004 when I was looking through photos from a vacation to Mexico. As I flipped through the pictures, one stood out. *Who is that in that bikini?* It was me, and I looked a hot mess. There I was, sitting on a horse wearing nothing but a bikini, my exposed thighs looking like boulders and my stomach hanging over the bikini bottom. To top it all off, I had the nerve to be oiled up and smiling. That was my *aha* moment (in my Oprah voice). I signed up for a boot camp fitness class and lost 30 pounds. I maintained the weight loss for about two years. Then, life happened again.

OH, IT'S ON!

Retiring from the Navy in 2010, I was in my second marriage and headed toward my second divorce. I was lost, confused, and gaining weight again. I can't say I was an emotional eater because I indiscriminately ate all the time. I stopped exercising, stopped caring, and just . . . stopped.

Although I was never diagnosed, I know I was depressed. My career was ending, my marriage was ending, and I thought my value was ending. My then (second) husband broke the news that he wanted a divorce over the phone . . . a week before my birthday . . . two weeks before I was scheduled to move back home with him and start our new life together after my retirement. I had given my 30-day notice to move out of my house, reserved the moving van, and turned down two job offers.

I remember very distinctly that Sunday afternoon when I talked to him on the phone. I was sitting in my car in the parking lot after church, and I called him to check in and talk for a bit. His mood was solemn, and I knew something was wrong. He finally said he didn't think he wanted to be married anymore and didn't think I should move back home. "I just have too much going on in my life right now," he said. I asked why, I cried and pleaded, and then, I ended the conversation and drove home. There, I had a nervous breakdown and two pity parties. My prayer to God was, "Father, if you wake me up from this, then I will know this was your plan."

When I opened my swollen eyes the next morning, it was on! I got back everything the devil tried to steal from me. The leasing office somehow lost my 30-day notice (God). The moving van cancellation fee was waived (God). I got a job (God). I joined my current church on my birthday (God). And I breathed for the first time in three years (God).

By 2012, I'd gained some of my weight back. Life was happening again. My grandmother, my queen, my girl . . . was starting her transition. She had been diagnosed with stomach cancer before, and since she'd beat it in the past, I thought she was in the clear. In October 2012, my grandmother was admitted to the hospital. The cancer had spread and at 93 years old she wasn't a candidate for surgery. The conversations about nursing homes and rehabilitation centers were quickly dismissed as my grandmother informed us all that she would die in her own home when she was ready. My aunts rotated their responsibility of care for my grandmother. They outfitted the house with beds and supplies, and when they discussed a bedside commode, my grandmother (who was weak and frail) promptly announced she would not be using the toilet next to her bed. She was "too jazzy for that!"

On December 20, 2012, I diagnosed myself as a diabetic. I felt tired, thirsty, and terrible at work. I called my doctor because I thought I had the classic symptoms of diabetes, but she assured me I was wrong as the bloodwork from my physical in August came back fine. After great persistence, my doctor agreed to see me that afternoon. I went in at about 3:00 p.m. My doctor took more tests and sent me back to the waiting room to await the results. She said if my results weren't back by 4:00 p.m., she would send me home to return in the morning. At 3:58 p.m., my doctor came out with her nurse and a wheelchair. She looked at me, and I knew. "You have diabetes," she said. A normal blood glucose range is 70–100; mine was 666. The wheelchair was my chariot to the ER, where I was admitted to the hospital. Had I gone home, I could have slipped into a diabetic coma and died. BUT GOD!

I was told it would take at least two to three days to get my levels normal. At that time, my son was serving in the United States Navy and deployed to Afghanistan. I was divorced and living alone while my family was hundreds of miles away from me. I was in the hospital for two days when the doctors decided to keep me over the weekend because my levels weren't where they wanted them to be. I was okay with that until my cousin called to tell me my grandmother's doctor suggested my family gather around her because she wasn't going to make it past the weekend. My heart sank. The doctor predicted Grandma would be gone by Christmas. That was my reality. I was in the hospital, my son was in Afghanistan, and my grandmother was dying. While my family gathered by my grandmother's bedside to say their goodbyes, I pleaded with my doctor to release me. She refused.

The earliest I could be released was the following Sunday, December 23rd. "I'm sorry," she said, "but based on your health, I'm afraid of something going wrong. There isn't anything I can do." I told her there was something I could do and asked her to start the paperwork to release me against medical advice (AMA). I told her to pack me up a bag of insulin and whatever else she needed to cover herself, but I was leaving that hospital. She tried to talk me out of it, but I signed out that Thursday afternoon, drove to Cleveland Friday morning, laid with my grandmother Friday and Saturday, then drove back to Chicago on Sunday. The next morning, on Christmas Eve, my grandmother passed away. *But God!*

It hasn't been easy, but I finally figured out this health/weight thing. I dropped from my heaviest to a size four. When the doctor threatens to cut off toes and fingers if you don't control your blood glucose levels, you may want to listen. I own too many shoes, and I'm far too cute to not be able to wear open-toe sandals. Everyone has different things to motivate them; mine was shoes. Although emotional trauma, disappointment, and aging caused me to take my health for granted, my diabetes diagnosis and grandmother's passing put my life in clear perspective for me.

Along this journey, I had to change my physical life by:

- Accepting the real consequences of an unhealthy diet and exercise program.

- Realizing diabetes won't stop me from living a ful-filled life, but if not managed, it will end my life.

- Saying no to working too much, giving too much, and trying to be too much for others.

- Focusing on myself and my health.

- Thinking about all the shoes I won't be able to wear if I have toes amputated.

UNPACK

I said no to eating half a box of Ho-Hos, no to eating at 10:00 p.m., and no to eating because food was available. I had to get up and run without the excuses of my hair, sweat, or gym shoes not matching my outfit. I said no to procrastinating about getting fit.

PACK

I said yes to reducing a whole box of Ho-Hos to three Ho-Hos. I said yes to me, finally. Through two divorces, the loss of my grandmother, my mother, and my eldest aunt, I realized I had strength to get through anything.

MAINTAIN AND NURTURE MY POLISH

I am the type of polished girl who leaves the shop and some-how finds a way to nick my nails (no matter how long I've left them under those lights with the air blowing on them). I notice it the moment it happens, and I either fix it or forget it. From a distance, you won't notice it. Even if you look at me long enough, you won't see it. It's only when I tell you my flaw and show it to you, that you'll become aware of it.

That's my approach now. I don't sweat the small stuff, but if it bothers me, I'll change it.

SEVEN POLISHED QUESTIONS:

1. **What advice would you give to women in a similar situation?**

   My advice about our health journey is it's yours. You won't get better until you want to. I pray it does not have to come to you being diagnosed with diabetes or any other medical conditions. But if it does, you must decide if you want to participate in living or start preparing to die.

2. **Knowing what you know now, what would you tell yourself at the start of this journey?**

   Step away from the plate, cancel the pity parties, stop feeling sorry for yourself and find yourself.

3. **What is your favorite beauty secret?**

   Running. It makes me sweat and glisten. It makes my cheeks flushed and red. It releases endorphins that make me feel wonderful. It also allows me to have personal time with myself and my thoughts. At the end of every run, I know I look and feel great.

4. **What is your favorite pampering secret?**

   A bubble bath with a diet coke, one or two Ho-Hos, and jazz music.

5. **As a woman, what is the best advice you have ever received?**

   When my grandmother announced she was not going to have a bedside commode because she was "too jazzy for that," she went on to say: "No matter what life throws at you, no matter what situation you find yourself in, and no matter how bad things get, remember what you are made of." She told me to remember I came from strong stock and that I will never be too far from jazzy.

6. **Are you polished right now?**

I am not perfectly polished, but the toes showing out of my peep toe shoes look fabulous.

7. **Is a woman's sanity directly linked to her pedicure? Why or Why not?**

I believe it is. Womanhood—and all that we are and do—is linked to how we feel and how we look. I mark my femininity daily in how I dress and how I act. It is often said that you can't judge someone on how they look. I disagree. In my opinion, my appearance is the first step to getting or wanting to know me. Therefore, the state of my pedicure shows you what I consider important in the story of *me*. On the days where my pedicure is jacked up, best believe it's not a good day.

Your Perspective

 Whose journey did you relate to the most? Why?

 Whose journey inspired you to move forward? Why?

 What emotions did you experience while reading these stories?

When / where did your journey begin?

What are you inspired to do?

THE HYPOTHESIS:
THE RUNDOWN

These stories are only a few of those shared with me over the years that helped to shape my hypothesis: *A woman's sanity is directly linked to her pedicure.* To unpack this a little more, let's look at each polished type again. Each woman gave a vivid account of their journey; they told their stories with bold stripes of color, sound, and imagery. What did you see and hear that would help you identify each woman's polished type? Who would you describe as layered, chipped, high polished, or wrecked? In your opinion, which of these women is perfectly polished (for her) or well on her way?

LAYERED

Remember, the layered woman wants you to believe that she is polished under the premise that if she looks polished . . . then she must be. This woman is driven by the busyness of it all and has a difficult time saying "No." She adds layer upon layer of activities, roles, responsibilities, and polish.

A few examples of Layered:

- I was most comfortable when I was busy; in fact, busyness comforted me when I miscarried two of my children.

- Monique was layered with everyone's opinion of who she should be and was being crushed under the weight of her fiancé's secret.

- Wendy and her husband layered their relationship with activities, sex and wigs to avoid addressing their lack of intimacy.

CHIPPED

For this woman, the stress of not saying "No" has gone too far and it shows. She is starting to resist and resent all the requests made of her and doesn't quite seem to be herself. She is the result of multi-tasking gone wrong.

A few examples of Chipped:

- Before totally wrecking her finances, Rebecca's budget was so fragmented she couldn't participate in family celebrations and events with her friends.

- Nichole's list of red flags was continually being tested as her perception of what her husband should be or do, and her own strength was challenged.

- After two marriages, two divorces, and on the verge of retiring, Debra's health, her perception of self and her future were undoubtedly tattered and frayed.

HIGH POLISHED

Ms./Mrs./Miss Thang has it going on . . . don't ever forget that. A high polished woman takes the Layered woman's need to appear perfect to a whole new level; she focuses on herself at all cost.

Two examples of High Polished:

- At some point, Kelly decided to make it all work . . . for her. She was so focused on her career and what she wanted that she risked her health by going back to work only eleven days after giving birth to twins.

- Believe it or not, Wendy's decision to throw caution to the wind and pursue an affair was a very High Polished thing to do.

WRECKED

She is my favorite polished type . . . perhaps because I have seen her looking back at me on many occasions as I stared into the bathroom mirror wondering, "What the hell happened?" Under the stress and pressure of life, this woman loosened her grip, opened her hands, and let it all go; she decided to do nothing to get back on track, nothing at all . . . at least for now.

Examples of the Wrecked type were revealed in each of our stories at some point:

- Avoiding my pain and disappointment eventually led to both emotional and physical trauma.

- Life comes at you fast. Rebecca learned a hard lesson when her finances quickly got out of hand.

- Monique crashed into depression and despair before she decided to rediscover who she was . . . who she truly was.

- Nichole thought she had a handy answer for everything, including miscarrying her first child.

- Kelly's need to pursue her desires (career and material things) eventually led to her wasting precious time with her kids and losing her beloved Mercedes.

- In the end, Wendy had to recover from a wrecked relationship with her then-husband and God, whose voice she'd ignored.

- Educated in health and fitness, Debra still suffered the blow of being diagnosed with the lifestyle disease diabetes at the same time as she had to face one of the most challenging losses of her life.

The journeys of these women often intersected between polished and layered, layered and chipped, or chipped and high polished. These stories also highlight three key assumptions.

ASSUMPTION 1

We are not simply one polished type. Although there may be one dominant type at any given time or even most of the time, we are all various degrees of multiple polished types along our journey. Now you may be saying, "Girl, I'm tired," and the thought of wrapping your mind around the various shades and degrees of polished is too much. I get it. The goal of the self-assessment and the stories was not to put you in a box (I hate boxes), but rather to illustrate how quickly and fluidly we transition from one polished type to another.

TRY THIS

Am I *Every* Woman? Consider the following:

- Describe a time when you felt balanced (based on your terms, not the opinion of others. Your *balanced* or *polished* may look crooked, tilted or lop-sided to me, but safely puts you first and works well for you).

- What can you glean from this experience that will help you maintain or re-establish your balance/ rhythm?

- Describe a time when you felt Layered, Chipped or Wrecked simultaneously, or in the same season.

You can be multiple shades of polished at the same time, or during the same journey; please be patient with you.

ASSUMPTION 2

Stress impacts our polished type. Stress and avoidance can accelerate us along the polished continuum, quickly moving us towards *wrecked* without warning or notice. To circumvent transitioning to High Polished or Wrecked . . . pause; stop; rest.

Life happens, but intentionally sit still with yourself. In the face of empowering messages that encourage women to GET all we can, and BE all we can, I want to give you a gift.

Are you ready? Here it is . . . I gift you permission to SLOW DOWN . . . STOP, if you have to. I just lost half of my readers and I don't even care.

Beloved, take care of you first and foremost. Sure, you have things to do and accomplish, but if you are too stressed and tired to enjoy it, what does it matter?

TRY THIS

Do absolutely nothing. You may say you can't afford to do nothing, but the truth is you can't afford to keep going at your current pace. I dare you (yea, I said it) to schedule the following:

- One hour doing absolutely nothing. Don't think about your plans or who needs you; merely sit in the window, the park or somewhere quiet and do nothing.

- Several quiet hours to complete the remaining activities and the One Last Thing section in this book.

- One full day of alone time. Go get a mani/pedi at a salon that truly pampers you (if they herd you in and out like a cow, you are in the wrong place). Then treat yourself to a facial and/or a massage, lunch and maybe a movie. Go for a run, take a dance or an art class. Do something all day by yourself.

Don't work over-time to catch up on your list of things to do. If this is your strategy, then you missed the point. I apologize, I should have read the fine print on the label of my gift. Permission granted to slow down may also put you in a position to bravely say, "No!" You're welcome.

ASSUMPTION 3

The art of unpacking and packing is an essential habit we must exercise if we are to get our polish together. Each woman identified something or some things they eliminated along their journey, and something or some things they picked up to help them along the way. Equal commitment must be given to both actions, and they must be seen as one task.

Early in my career I traveled quite a bit. Although I had my standard packed items (soap, toothpaste, toothbrush, cologne, comfy shoes, etc.), each trip required me to go through the grueling task of considering what I needed for that specific occasion. It would have been easier to pack one bag and take it with me every time, but it doesn't work that way. Every time I refused to unpack my luggage when I got home from a trip, it caused me more effort and energy when it was time to travel again. Because I couldn't throw all of my newly selected items on top of what was chosen for the last trip, I had to unpack then pack again.

I'm sure you know where I'm going with this. "Bag lady, you gone hurt your back . . . dragging all them bags like that." Learning when to say "No" to people, places, things and requests is often painful and uncomfortable, especially if you've been carrying them around for a long time, or if your need to be needed has made you the perfect people-pleasing martyr. You must consistently consider and unpack whatever becomes a hindrance; with equal consistency, consider and pack that which will be useful each unique leg of your journey.

TRY THIS

- What are you excited to unpack or say "No" to, and why?

- What do you need to unpack but the thought of doing so makes you nervous? Why is that?

Unpacking is freeing, liberating, and necessary. Packing requires being humble enough to seek assistance and maybe even trying something new.

- What are you excited to pack and why?

- What do you need to pack, but the thought of doing so makes you nervous? Why is that?

Whether you agree with the hypothesis or not, stay with me. Part III of this book explores five categories that have a direct impact on your polish.

PART THREE

YOUR JOURNEY STARTS HERE

GET YOUR POLISH TOGETHER

"The journey between what you once were and who you are now becoming is where the dance of life really takes place."

—Barbara De Angelis

Have you considered if you are perfectly polished for your lifestyle and ready to share your story of encouragement with other women? Or do you still have a little work to do? Either way, to help you start your journey toward becoming (or staying) polished, this section is designed to help you find your rhythm by determining what elements of your life may need to be stabilized and polished up.

Keep in mind, polished is not about a moment in time. It cannot be completely defined by anyone outside of you, nor does it ignore that you are a complex and multifaceted creature. Whether you're polished, totally wrecked, or some strange, yet wonderful amalgamation of all the polished types, take a moment to determine what elements of your life may be a place of extended stress.

As I mentioned before, regardless of the season I was in (polished, layered, chipped, etc.), five manageable categories emerged over the span of my journey. Because these categories seemed to be common themes amongst the many women I spoke with (as evident by the stories in the previous section), I studied them individually to determine what polished would look like for me. (I was sick and tired of being sick and tired.) Allow me to define each category, then you're off to map out your own journey toward becoming polished.

EMOTIONAL &
SPIRITUAL

Although the rest of the categories are randomly presented, I listed this one first because, in my opinion, it has become the lynchpin for all the others. If my emotional and spiritual life is out of whack (or chipped), eventually everything will falter. Do you command peace, or do you just hope for it?

This category is about your ability to stay calm and focused, even when all hell breaks loose. The emotional and spiritual category is defined by your ability to get anchored in a place where purpose, vision, and peace flow abundantly. It is your higher ground. When everything and everyone around you is out of control, this connection will re-ground you and remind you of your values and the mission you set out to accomplish. For some, this is an internal connection with themselves or perhaps conviction to a particular religion. For others, it is an intimate relationship with a higher power in whom they can trust, cast their cares upon, and extend incomprehensible faith.

Where do you go and what do you do to systematically get centered? (Ladies, an apple martini is not the right answer.) Success in this category does not mean you are not affected by stress. As a matter of fact, it is vital you do not fake it or falsely portray stability in this category.

Emotional and spiritual success means you can maintain peace and some sense of joy even when hell itself wants to challenge you. This category speaks to your ability to stay grounded with your feet firmly planted even when a whirlwind of mishaps hit you. This is about your resolve to focus on the big picture and the possibility that tomorrow will be a blessing when today feels/seems/looks like crap.

Researchers in the field of psychoneuroimmunology (PNI) study the effects the mind has on our health and resistance to disease. PNI research suggests that emotional and mental stress can lead to anxiety, cognitive (thinking) problems, personality changes, behavior problems, and a sustained feeling of low energy or depression. It is entirely natural to experience a wide range of moods in everyday life; however, sustained unaddressed and unmanaged stress may lead to fatigue, appetite changes, restlessness and irritability, withdrawal from pleasurable activities, and feelings of hopelessness and helplessness.

A few examples of when the emotional and spiritual side of you is out of whack:

- You are easily angered; you're mad and you don't know why.

- Your attempts to fill that feeling of emptiness are continuously unsuccessful. Neither relationships, sex, alcohol, food, exercise, projects, children, church, nor promotions seem to satisfy you for long.

- High levels of sustained stress cause you to experience feelings of worthlessness, self-hate, and guilt; you have trouble sleeping at night and often experience an inability to make decisions.

- You allow the busyness of your schedule to interfere with your relationship with God; you lose your passion for prayer or alone time with Him. This happened to me a lot.

- Monique depended upon praise and approval to provide internal peace and personal satisfaction only to experience emotional and spiritual turmoil as a result.

- Debra was emotionally strained after her second divorce and the loss of her grandmother; it took her a while to overcome the physical ramifications of these emotional experiences.

What do you consistently do to lay hold of and maintain your peace?

TRY THIS

Breathe. You may be thinking, *I know how to breathe.* Or you may have never given breathing any thought because we do it naturally. Remember when you were a kid and tried to hold your breath for a long time? Eventually, the **need** to breathe overpowered your **will** not to breathe. Even if you won the "I can hold my breath longer than you can" challenge and passed out, your brain took over and your lungs gasped for the air they needed. Your desire or **will** to win may have made you the victor, but your body's basic **needs** won . . . and they will always win. This fundamental principle is true for your emotional health and your spirit. They will suffer without air . . . without breath . . . and without life. It may sound crazy, but schedule time to BREATHE. You don't need an entirely serene and candlelit environment to breathe. You can breathe even when some crazy person is provoking thoughts of you punching them in the face.

Simply . . .

- Inhale through your nose for four complete seconds

- Hold your breath for four complete seconds

- Exhale through your mouth for four complete seconds

- Repeat the cycle until you begin to feel a sense of stillness and serenity

Repeat this exercise several times daily. I often start my day this way. Expect this to be uncomfortable at first. I literally felt like I was dying the first time I tried this technique. You will eventually feel a sense of control and peace. As this methodology becomes easy for you, take your skills to the next level by scheduling a few pampering moments daily to meditate on scriptures or positive mantras while you are breathing in this manner. Could you benefit from more peace? How can you establish the peace you need? BREATHE. Your emotions and your spirit will thank you.

Your goal in this category should be to manage internal turmoil by creating the kind of inner peace that stands flat-footed in the face of mayhem. Success in this category does not mean avoiding emotions, stress, or experiences that stretch you outside of your comfort zone. As a matter of fact, getting out of your comfort zone and leaning into new experiences are required; just remember to fight to hold on to your peace and the assurance you will survive.

Self-Identity

Many studies have been conducted to unravel the connection between stress, self-esteem, and depression. (Translation: how you see yourself impacts your stress level and sustained stress may also influence how you define who you are.) In as much, one of the ways to handle stress is by becoming more confident and self-assured. When you feel great about yourself and have a positive outlook, you manage stress and pressure more effectively.

So, here is my question, who do you say that you are? Most women identify with—and define themselves by—the roles they have (e.g., wife, mother, daughter, sister, auntie, friend, frenemy, leader, neighbor, etc.). The self-identity category is narrower and more defined. Instead of focusing on the role you play, the heart of the matter is how you function in that role and how you would describe yourself. For example, I am a **passionate** training professional, an **active** leader in my church, a **loving**, **understanding** and incredibly **sexy** wife, a **creative** author, and a **driven** CEO. Who and what do you allow to influence or define who you are?

How many times have you said or heard your girlfriends say, "I am a horrible *(fill in the blank)*" all because the food was burned, the bills weren't paid, a special event was forgotten, the house was messy, or because of some other mishap? Many opportunities will present themselves as evidence we're wrecked or less than what God says we are. These perceived failures not only exasperate undue stress, but over time, they negatively impact our self-esteem and how we see ourselves.

The uniqueness of this category is both its challenge and its strength. It does not look at past evidence or the opinion of others, no matter how valid. Self-identity is a life-long journey. Your success in this category is contingent upon your commitment to finding out who you really are and identifying with the woman you were created to be.

I see myself as passionate, active, loving, understanding, sexy, inspiring, creative, and driven. I look for evidence to support my vision of myself (what I say, what I do), and if I do not find the proof, I create it! There is a personal caution here: be careful not to overinflate your self-image. Because I see myself as strong and unbreakable, I often experience symptoms and signs of acute Superwoman Syndrome. I am sure you are very familiar with women with an invisible *S* on their chests who do entirely too much for too long.

A few examples that may reveal your self-identity as chipped:

- You still feel guilt and shame about what someone did to you; somehow their actions have shaped how you see yourself.

- You don't believe you deserve the best because your behavior and decisions in the past (even your recent past) were not responsible, pleasant, or perhaps even legal.

- You compare yourself to others and often envy their perceived success.

- You secretly compare your body shape, size, and personal style to your friend who reaches her physical goals before you do. Then, you publicly make "innocent" snide remarks about her. (You, my dear, are what we call a hater.)

- Instead of dealing with your emotions, you over-achieve in everything you do. You feel compelled to do more and be more. This was so me.

- Rebecca hid her private financial situation in order to live publicly as though she had it all together.

- Monique allowed others to determine how she should behave and even who she should be in order to fit into a lifestyle. This kind of pressure cannot be sustained.

- Nichole thought she had to live up to her vision of the perfect mother, wife, and administrative assistant, and wanted her husband to live up to her list.

- Kelly believed that compared to the image she had of her mom, she was a lousy mother to her children; conversely, she was obsessed with her vision of success and how she wanted others to perceive her.

Regardless of your spiritual background or religion, the Judeo-Christian faith depicts one of the strongest illustrations of what I'm trying to describe here, and it started in the Garden of Eden. Adam was created to have dominion over the land and the animals. Through a series of events, he was presented with Eve as his wife and helpmeet. In disobedience, they ate the forbidden fruit from the tree of life and death, and instantly, they became ashamed of their nakedness and hid. God asked Adam two simple questions:

- Where are you?

- Who told you that you were naked?

Because of circumstances and failure to meet an expectation, Adam completely forgot what he was created for and the authority that was given to him. And in his shame, he ran and hid.

In an attempt to help you realize that you, the real you, are more than what you have done or who others say that you are, I have a few questions to ask you:

- Woman, where are you? (Are you where you want to be?)

- Who told you that you were naked? (Who or what have you allowed to define you?)

- How do you see yourself? How do you present yourself to the world?

- Who do you say that you are?

TRY THIS

Who Do I Say That I Am? Look in the mirror. What adjectives would you use to describe you? What characteristics do you like, or even love, about yourself?

- Get a stopwatch. Within 15 seconds, call out all of the positive adjectives you can think of that describe who you are. Make sure you're calling out positive adjectives (i.e., dynamic, funny, exciting, emotional, confident), not roles that you play (i.e., mother, wife, executive, etc.). You should be able to call out 17 or more adjectives in 15 seconds. GO!

How challenging was this activity? Why? Did you have to resist calling out negative attributes? Why?

- Spend a few pampering moments in the mirror and tell yourself how wonderful you are every day.

The objective of Self-Identity is to establish an accurate view of yourself that safely puts you first while encouraging you to be the best version of *you* that you can be.

PHYSICAL

I know, I know . . . did I have to go there? Yes, my love, I did. As mentioned before, headaches, low libido, high blood pressure, and weight gain are examples of the physical effects stress has on our bodies. These are unsavory manifestations of our bodies expressing *dis-ease*. The truth is, how we feel affects how we think about ourselves . . . and vice versa.

Women are beautiful. Whether we are tall, short, skinny, muscular, curvaceous, or voluptuous, we all have the right to love that utterly naked woman that looks back at us in the mirror. Here is the problem: many believe what a small minority tells us to believe about our shape and size. Therefore, no matter how fierce, vibrant, and beautiful that woman looking back at us is, she is always flawed.

This physical category is not about losing 20 pounds. It is distinctively about making a conscious effort to present the best physical woman you can be. It is not about the tape measure alone, but other vital measurements as well. What are your systolic and diastolic numbers (blood pressure)? Do you have high cholesterol? Are you pre-diabetic? Are you anorexic or bulimic? Does your love for dairy trigger inflammation and make you a prime candidate for arthritis?

Those are the deep questions, but here are a few more that are telling as well. What is your personal style? Do your clothes communicate your self-worth? (This is not a money question. I couldn't care less about how much you spent on those Louis Vuitton shoes, especially if your pedicure is jacked up.) What are your hair, clothes, and makeup saying about you, and is that what you meant to communicate? This category is triangulated; it speaks to your physical fitness, your medical health, and the outward presentation of it all.

A few physical examples that indicate this category may be a challenge for you:

- You honestly believe you don't have time to make and keep a doctor's appointment.

- You experience a plethora of physical effects of stress like headaches, skin rashes, nerve twitches in your face, high blood pressure, weight gain, weight loss, etc.

- You start a new healthy lifestyle every dang Monday.

- You know you do not dress appropriately for your age, body shape, or size. You know you badly need a makeover but cannot figure out where to start.

- I ignored my physical health and the effects of stress for years. It wasn't until my body sent warning signal after warning signal did I slow down, pay attention, and began to give my body the love I needed, and deserved.

- Wendy suspects improperly dealing with her stressful marriage for so long finally resulted in a deadly prognosis.

- Debra did not get a hold of the emotional turmoil she was experiencing before it began to manifest in her health.

What do you consistently do to appreciate and take care of the physical woman you are today?

TRY THIS

Get Naked. I can hear some of you grumbling, "Ugh, anything but that." While others of you are already butt-booty naked yelling, "What's next? Will there be toys involved?" Regardless of which end of the spectrum you rest, it is important to embrace your physical woman as she is today so that you can make and sustain positive changes tomorrow.

- Stand in front of a full-length mirror.

- Starting with your hair, your forehead, your eyes, your nose, your cheeks, your lips, and then your neck, say to each body part, one by one, "Hello, beautiful *(name the body part you are addressing)*. I am so blessed to have you."

- Now take off all your clothes, one piece at a time.

- As each piece of clothing falls to the floor, tell the revealed body part(s), "Hello, beautiful *(name the body part you are addressing)*. I am so blessed to have you."

- Repeat this step until you are completely naked, and all your body parts have heard you honor them.

- Now tell that beautiful, naked woman in the mirror that you . . .

  - Love and appreciate her, just the way she is. (Keep saying it, you'll get there.)

  - Will take greater care of her from this moment forward.

- Will eat what is healthy for her and will exercise to keep her strong.

- Will drape her with clothes that flatter her shape and communicate to the world how fabulous she is.

- Will seek medical expertise to ensure she gets and remains as healthy as possible.

  Yes, dear, you should eventually schedule a doctor's appointment. You cannot allow your life to become so layered with activities, work, and taking care of others that you don't have time to take care of you. When was the last time you had a pap smear or a mammogram?

- Will pamper her more often.

Your physical strategy should ensure you are healthy, physically strong, and your outward appearance comfortably aligns with the beautiful, polished woman you are.

RELATIONAL

How many of the people who are important to you . . . have found your last nerve . . . and are firmly standing on it? Ask too much of you? Do not include you? Pressure you to do things you do not want to do?

Relationships present another glorious opportunity to experience stress from time to time. Relationship stress can happen with our spouse, parents, children, siblings, friends, neighbors, jobs, co-workers, employees, bosses, and even total strangers.

The relational category is about developing and maintaining relationships that honor you and positively support who you say that you are. The frame of your relationships (i.e., wife, mother, daughter, BFF, employee, etc.) is far less critical than the actual content or quality of the specific relationship. Consider your relationships as bank accounts. The more deposits made, the more valuable the accounts become, and the less likely a withdrawal or two will jeopardize the accounts' total worth. The maintenance and upkeep of these relationship accounts is not solely your responsibility. As a matter of fact, each relationship is a joint account and is the collective responsibility of both you and the other individual.

If you consistently made $10 deposits in your checking account—every week for one year—and then attempted to make a $20 withdrawal only to be told you had insufficient funds, what would you do? Clearly someone was making withdrawals all along and depleted the account, or the bank is in error. Either way, I'm sure if this became a reoccurring theme, you would limit or eliminate the other person's access to the account or terminate your relationship with the bank.

Why then do we tolerate and even participate in misappropriation of funds when it comes to our relationships? What is more important: your money or you? This category is defined by your ability to establish and nurture healthy relationships with the people in your life without sacrificing your joy, peace, love, sanity, or any of the other four categories. Simply cutting people out of your life is NOT a viable strategy. Most importantly, this category is also about developing a healthy relationship with yourself without going overboard and establishing a guarded, self-absorbed, high polished attitude. When was the last time you spent some quality time alone with your thoughts, your hopes, and your dreams?

A few relational examples to consider:

- You don't stand up to the person/people that continually speak harshly to you; instead, you maintain a relationship that doesn't make you feel valued or appreciated.

- You shrink and pretend not to be as fabulous, funny, or intelligent in order to make others (e.g., spouse, friends, family, boss, etc.) feel good about themselves.

- You don't spend any one-on-one time with yourself.

- You stay at a job because you're afraid to be rejected by future, potential employers.

- Nichole realized her relationship with her lists was not sustainable; she decided to put her marriage first in order to find her rhythm and establish peace.

- Kelly put her career above everything, believing this relationship (and the relationship she had with her Mercedes) would bring her the security, comfort, and esteem she desired.

- Wendy knew she would never get the emotional deposits she needed from Robert but proceeded to marry him anyway.

How do you ensure your relationships are mutually beneficial?

TRY THIS

Count the Cost. Are your current relationships adding value to who you say that you are and assisting in pampering your self-image? Or have you unknowingly surrounded yourself with people who consistently drain you emotionally and mentally without regularly making positive deposits into your life?

- What is the value of your relationships?

  - Use the Relationship Value Table below to assess your key relationships. In the first column, list the names of four individuals you currently interact with regularly. (Consider assessing your relationship with your job.)

  - In the second column, rate each of the relationships on a scale from 0–10, with 10 being most satisfying, and 0 suggesting you don't feel honored in the relationship (nor supported for who you say that you are).

- Rate your relationship with yourself (YOU) as well. To what degree do you honor yourself? Is your negative self-talk overwhelming and demeaning?

RELATIONSHIP VALUE TABLE

Name	Satisfaction Rating	Relationship Type
YOU		

- Let's stick with our bank account analogy. Consider each relationship, then identify and write the Relationship Type in the third column. Use the descriptions below:

    - 10–8 range: **Preferred Account.** What will it take from both of you to maintain or improve your relationship value by 1 point?

    - 7–5 range: **Account Alert.** What will it take from both of you to move your relationship to an 8 or at least improve your relationship value by 1 point?

    - 0–4 range: **Insufficient Funds.** What will it take from both of you to increase the value of this relationship, or is it time to close this account?

- Pamper your spirit by scheduling and spending some quality time with your Preferred Account relationships. How can you strengthen these relationships? My greatest desire for you is that you have included yourself in this category.

- If by chance YOU fell within the 0–4 range, it is time to focus on the best thing you have going . . . yourself.

  - Review the *Emotional & Spiritual* and the *Self-Identity* sections again. Complete the breathing and "Who do you say that you are" exercises daily.

  - Above all, seek professional counseling if necessary. There is no shame or embarrassment in getting well. No amount of nail polish on your toes or body butter slathered on your skin is going to get to the root cause of how you are feeling toward yourself. Let me say it again here, "You are fearfully and wonderfully made. God has a plan for your life, and He loves you greatly."

- Do the Work. You most likely didn't need an assessment to identify those relationships that can be classified as an *Account Alert* or *Insufficient Funds*. Let's face it, you may have gotten to the answers quicker if I simply asked, "Who gets on your last *dang* nerve?" Your next step, perhaps the most important one, is to do the necessary work to improve these relationships and minimize the related stress.

The thought of working on this category may seem overwhelming, but keep this African proverb in mind, "It takes a village to raise a child." What happened to your village as you matured into an adult? Did it grow? Did it shrink? Most likely, many of the faces and their level of influence changed. Perhaps even the location of your village is different. Regardless of what remained the same and what changed, you still need a village—a group of people who support you, guide you, and are invested in your success.

If I could add to this proverb, it would be, "Yes, it takes a village to raise a child, but now that you're an adult, cultivate your own!" Your relationship goals should ensure you establish and nurture relationships that support who you say you are. Build relationships that are symbiotic and mutually beneficial.

FINANCIAL

Everyone wants more money. Stop lying if you say you don't. Money will make all things right, right? WRONG. A healthy relationship with our finances is a must. If you hit the lottery today, would your personal worth and value also increase? If you lose everything tomorrow, would you no longer be fearfully and wonderfully made; do you cease to have value, purpose, and significance?

You are not your money, and your money is not you. However, finances do play a role in establishing an abundant life. While your credit score doesn't define you, it does communicate to the financial world what you may think about money and the value of credit. It is used to identify your level of financial culpability. Perhaps the noise of your daily, weekly, or monthly budget is drowning out any concern for your credit score. Or maybe your credit score has taken a hit because your bills are late . . . not because you didn't have the funds, but because you were too busy to pay them (I am very familiar with this scenario).

This category defines the degree to which you have developed financial acumen, consistent responsibility, and a healthy respect for money and credit. Former financial reporter and author of *Zero Debt: The Ultimate Guide to Financial Freedom*, Lynette Khalfani-Cox wrote, "I was living above my means . . . The true costs of debt and financial problems aren't only the interest rate you're paying to Mastercard or Visa. The true cost is the toll that it's taking on your life and your relationships."

Debt stress is real, y'all! If not addressed, women who experience anxiety around finances and debt suffer from a range of stress-related illnesses including ulcers, migraines, back pain, anxiety, and unfortunately much more. A few examples that highlight the need to focus on financial stability:

- You are currently living paycheck to paycheck; not receiving one or two paychecks at all or receiving a few paychecks beneath your current salary would be financially devastating.

- You are afraid to answer the phone . . . it might be them!

- You don't know your credit score and keep poor financial records.

- You wake up in the middle of the night worried about bills and creditors.

- Rebecca was enjoying life so much, she went broke, then pretended her simple lifestyle was intentional.

- Kelly put her finances and her children's college funds at risk to portray an elite financial status.

- Wendy put financial security over her need for emotional connection.

Are you truly prepared for tomorrow? Have you done all you can to ensure you're well taken care of 10, 20, 30 years from now?

TRY THIS

Retire . . . *today!* When I was about five years old, my mother asked me what I wanted to be when I grew up. I innocently responded, "I want to be retired like Great Grandma Butler." Although everyone laughed, and my mother feared I might end up a lazy bumpkin, considering retirement early and often is a good habit.

- If you are not already retired, envision your retirement party.

  - Where is it? Who is there?

  - How are your family and friends celebrating you? What kind of music is playing?

  - How is the room decorated?

  - Is the party catered? Is there family-style serving?

  - What will happen the very next day?

- Download one of those phone apps that age any picture you upload (e.g., Aging Booth, age-me.com, Face of the Future, etc.). Take a picture of yourself, then take a deep breath and upload it to the app. Once the app has aged your image to 75 years or older, spend some time with your retired self.

  - If you do not make any changes to your financial acumen or habits, what kind of lifestyle can you promise your 75-year-old self?

  - What kind of polished lifestyle would you like to provide your 75-year-old self? How will you pamper her?

  - What can you do now to ensure you'll have the necessary resources then?

Your goal in this category should be to eliminate all financial stress by eliminating debt, increasing your savings, and eventually building wealth.

All five categories must work together. Although none of them is more important than the others, you may find one category has a greater impact on your sense of stability. For example, my emotional and spiritual life is the lynchpin or the glue that keeps me together. For others, their most impactful category may be physical or financial. As a note of caution, be careful not to tie everything to something you only participate in but do not ultimately have control over. For instance, if you make the physical category your primary focus, be sure that does not mean all other categories suffer until you reach your ideal weight. Be sure it doesn't mean nothing else matters if you fall ill. If you make the financial category your lynchpin, make sure you're prepared for unexpected events like a recession.

The next section will help you prioritize your polished categories and set the route for your polished journey.

GET STARTED!

Now that you have experienced each category and have a better understanding of what they mean, it's time to map out your initial polished journey by identifying both your strengths and your opportunities. To do so, follow the five steps outlined on the subsequent pages.

STEP ONE

Use the following point values to complete this portion of your polished journey:

A = 4 points
B = 3 points
C = 2 points
D = 1 point
E = 0 points

Refer to your responses from The Polished Assessment™ in Part I of this book. Now complete the Polished Assessment™ Scorecard below by writing the corresponding point value for each of your responses within each category of the assessment (Emotional & Spiritual, Self-Identity, Physical, Relational, and Financial). For example, if you answered question 6 of the assessment with an A response, then write the number 4 on the line provided in the Emotional & Spiritual category, for question 6, and so on.

For example:

Emotional & Spiritual

6. _4_
7. _3_
11. _0_
17. _4_
23. _1_

Total Category Points = _12_

POLISHED ASSESSMENT™ SCORECARD

Emotional & Spiritual

6. _____	7. _____	11. _____
17. _____	23. _____	
	Total Category Points = _____	

Self Identity

1. _____	8. _____	13. _____
18. _____	21. _____	
	Total Category Points = _____	

Physical

4. _____	14. _____	19. _____
22. _____	24. _____	
	Total Category Points = _____	

Relational

2. _____	3. _____	9. _____
12. _____	16. _____	
	Total Category Points = _____	

Financial

5. _____	10. _____	15. _____
20. _____	25. _____	
	Total Category Points = _____	

STEP TWO

Answer the questions below to further define your polished journey:

    A. What is your highest scoring category(ies)?

          _____. This is your area(s) of **strength**.

    B. What is your lowest scoring category(ies)?

          _____. This is your area(s) of **opportunity**.

STEP THREE

Rank your categories from lowest score (First) to highest score (Fifth). This is the route or order you should follow as you begin to work through your strategy:

First:

Second:

Third:

Fourth:

Fifth:

The fourth step is to write out your vision declarations. Before we get to step four, capture your perspective on the next page.

Your Perspective

What surprised you about your results?

Which "Try this" activity was most meaningful and impactful? Why?

What makes knowing your area(s) of strength and your area(s) of development powerful?

What are you inspired to do?

STEP FOUR

Write the vision and make it plain. Yes, the next step is to define and write your vision of polished. Why bother writing it down? I'm glad you asked.

DID YOU KNOW?

Forbes conducted a study on goal setting carried out by Harvard MBA Program graduates. Only three percent of the graduates developed written goals while in the program; however post-graduation, this small minority was earning, on average, ten times as much as the remaining ninety-seven percent of the class combined. These graduates understood the power of written goals and their connection to accountability; perhaps their written goals became the impetus of what inspired them to keep moving forward. Translation . . . let's start writing ladies.

Now that you have identified your strengths and opportunities with regards to the polished categories, and you've ranked them to determine how you should map out your journey, it is important to define what polished looks like **for you**. Remember, polished will look different for each of us and you will most likely refine your vision over time.

After many years of struggling to define polished for myself and delving deep into each of these categories, I determined *my* Perfectly Polished meant the pace of my life must encourage self-care and allow me to give each category time and attention. In brief, my personal vision is as follows:

Emotional & Spiritual

- I am God's Daughter. I do all things through Him that strengthens me.

Identity

- I am God's Daughter, therefore the power of my tongue brings life, death and encouragement, for God Himself has given me an instructed tongue to know the word that sustains the weary.

- Because I am God's Daughter I am fearfully and wonderfully made. I am fun, adventurous, accomplished, passionate, active, loving, understanding, sexy, inspiring, creative, intelligent, fierce and driven . . . and I know this full well.

Physical

- As God's Daughter I receive and I walk in Divine Health and Healing; for Jehovah Raphe has healed me, and He alone has made me whole. I decree and declare I am healthy, strong, and physically fit.

Relational

- As God's Daughter I possess the Peace of God, therefore I am at peace with myself and those around me. My village is forward-thinking, forward moving, and reinforces who I say that I am.

Financial

- I am God's Daughter; therefore, I decree and declare I am debt-free, wealthy, and generous with my resources.

Now am I all these things, all the time? NO WAY! Are there moments, specifically Saturday mornings, when you will catch me with my hair stuffed under a hat, wearing some dirty jeans or an old sweat suit? Well of course (so if you see me, don't post my picture on the internet with the caption "Look who's not so polished"). To ensure I keep moving forward, especially in those moments and seasons when I am completely sidetracked, chipped or even wrecked, I made sure I created *declarations* of my vision instead of neutral statements or even affirmations.

To write my vision was one thing, but to declare my vision is something else . . . something far more powerful. Most of my vision declarations are rooted in scripture. This is how I ensure I am focused on—and my words are aimed at—the abundant life God promised me. It is with these declarations I charge the atmosphere around me, settle my mind about what I will accomplish, and focus my daily efforts toward my desired end.

Trust me, there have been many stressful opportunities that required me to take control of myself and the atmosphere around me and declare, *"I am God's Daughter. I can do all things through Him that strengthens me. I am at peace with myself and those around me."* Did I get it right the first time? Naw, not even the first 100 times. It took me a while to get into the habit of declaring my vision before my mind and my behavior followed. I experienced the discomfort of cognitive dissonance along my journey because I needed, and still need, to verbalize my vision. Cognitive dissonance is the mental stress or discomfort experienced when our beliefs don't match our behaviors; eventually, something will change. We will either change our minds, thoughts, values, and beliefs, or change our behavior.

I'll give you a quick personal example. I'm pretty funny. No need to agree or disagree, it's just the truth. I used to think a part of what made me so funny was my command and brilliant placement of cuss words. As I grew in my relationship with Christ, it became painfully clear I had to walk away from this talent, this gift I'd crafted. Doing so, I feared I wouldn't be as funny. Many, many years later, I still find myself driving down the highway, or standing in line at Starbucks behind the last person in America that hasn't figured out that *tall*, *grande*, and *venti* translate to small, medium and large, or I may be conversing with someone who's trying my last nerve, and I have to declare, "I am God's daughter. I speak good words rather than worthless ones. The power of my words brings life, death and encouragement. For God has given me an instructed tongue to know the word that sustains the weary." I do not, I repeat, I DO NOT CUSS (not since page 33; Monique cussed on her own).

This is the same declaration I make when I'm nervous about speaking engagements or ministering to someone who has trusted me with something very personal and is looking for encouragement. After making such a powerful declaration, the words with which I choose to express myself, my confidence, and my behavior begin to line up accordingly.

To continue to map out your journey, it is vital you establish a vision or a desired end for your efforts as well. Each of the women who shared their stories had a different vision that

> CREATE VISION DECLARATIONS THAT STAND UP AND WALK AND PUSH YOU FORWARD, EVEN WHEN YOU WANT TO QUIT

inspired them to keep moving forward. Take a moment to review each category again and your reactions to the *Try This* activities. Then, define polished for yourself by creating a declaration for each category. Make them powerful. You do not have to anchor yours in scripture but do create vision declarations that will stand up and walk (as the Word became flesh and dwelt amongst us); declarations that will charge the atmosphere, change your mind, mood and attitude, and push you forward, even when you want to quit. Describe your ideal future. What do you see? What do you hear?

Emotional & Spiritual

•

Self-Identity

•

Physical

•

Relational

•

Financial

•

Try This

Declare something. Now that you have written your vision, it's time to declare it.

1. Reference the route of polished categories you identified through your assessment (see page 143).

2. Starting with your first category (your lowest score), read your vision declaration aloud repeatedly until you feel empowered and charged by your words.

    You may find it necessary to strengthen your declaration to ensure it inspires you to keep moving forward.

3. Repeat this process with each declaration until you are confident you have the most powerful, motivating, and charged declarations.

4. Commit to writing and declaring your first vision for the next 30 days. Then repeat with the next vision declaration, and so on.

I revisit my vision declarations frequently to ensure they are as powerful, inspiring, and forward-moving as possible. I take time to intentionally decompress, de-stress, and pamper myself.

So how can you make time to pamper yourself and embrace the life you deserve? Who or what must you unpack and finally say no to? Throughout the *One Last Thing* section, you will find a few basic strategies you may want to implement.

Technically this is the end of *Are You Polished?*; however, the remaining portion is dedicated to helping you commit to and achieve your polished goals. Remember, be patient; this is not a quick fix. Setting goals and getting polished is about your evolution and who you are becoming.

My Letter to You

GIRLFRIEND / LADYBUG / BABY GIRL / MA'AM!

I celebrate you for finishing. I hope you found this book insightful and necessary. It was important to me to not only write a book, but also to create an experience that would encourage you to safely put yourself first. I have found that polished means pampered *and* moving to a healthy rhythm that works for me; obviously, it is more than *just* a pedicure. However, I still believe a woman's pedicure reveals the degree to which she pampers herself and effectively manages everything on her plate (particularly in those five categories).

As I write this letter, I cannot help but think of my own journey and how long it took me to finish writing *Are You Polished?* As I stated before, it started as my tongue-in-cheek way to give busy women permission to pamper themselves more often; however, something happened along the way. I got too busy to finish the book I was writing to encourage you not to be too busy. Geesh! I became layered (my comfort zone), chipped, and even wrecked. I thought I disqualified myself. I thought I had to have it all together before I could say anything to you. I thought you would see me as a hypocrite if I wasn't perfectly polished all the time.

Then, all the stories started to come in, and I was moved by their honesty and transparency. How could I be anything

151

less? A wise woman admonished me to think of my readers and the excuse I would give them for procrastinating. She told me to take a polaroid picture of every woman to whom I thought this book would be a blessing. I took lots of pictures, but since I don't know many of you, I imagined our divine meeting instead. What would I say? Would I try to fake perfection, or would I tell the truth? I figured you, like me, had heard enough lies and make-believe stories, so I decided to finish the assignment God gave me.

I also began to see the value of my entire journey, even the detours and delays. It's because of these moments I am stronger and actively pursuing the abundant life God promised. He would not let the vision die. Every time I walked away from this book or ran from my imaginary conversation with you, God reminded me (with restless nights and this unexplainable flutter in my belly) I was on assignment, and I had to give birth to this *baby* I'd carried for years. Commercial break: Baby Girl, finish it . . . whatever it is.

As mentioned a few times throughout this book, the content is not intended to address mental illness in any form. If you find yourself in need of professional counseling, I pray you will pursue and embrace the treatment you need.

Let's recap. You have your polished type and your polished journey mapped out (the order of your categories). You also have your vision declarations to charge you and the atmosphere around you. While I am pleased you have made it this far, it is not my desire to leave you here. If you need a little more, the *One Last Thing* section is for you.

Take a day or so (but not too long) to reflect on this experience, then turn to page 157 and resolve to take the additional steps. Create an action plan that keeps you moving forward. In the meantime, go for a walk, run, dance, snuggle up with a good book, enjoy a good meal; take a hike, a dip in the ocean, lake, stream, river or pool; meditate, stretch, worship, pray, sing off key as loud as you can; craft, sew, knit, write . . . do whatever it takes to pamper your feminine spirit . . . then . . . go get your toes done!

I want to hear from you and encourage you along the way. Don't wait until you get polished to write me. Feel free to email me at **thepolishedjourney@yahoo.com**. Maybe one day, you too will selflessly share your story and be the encouragement other women need to get their polish together.

Keep moving forward, my friend! Always,

Patrice

P.S. I almost forgot, in case you don't like to travel alone, or if you travel in a pack, discussion questions are provided towards the very end of this book to help you host your own Polished Party™ with a group of your friends. ENJOY, and email me the pics!

PART FOUR

ONE LAST THING

THIS IS YOUR BONUS TRACK

It's not that I want more shoes, it's just that they keep making them in my size.

—Unknown

But wait! There's more! Now that your vision has been cast and you are committed to pampering yourself more often, you are better positioned to capture the life you deserve. It is unrealistic to believe you will be polished during every season of your life, all the time. You will have to adjust along the way. The beauty of establishing your vision and your initial strategy is you will always have a place to return and start again, if necessary.

So, where do you go from here?

With your vision firmly in place, the final section of this book is appropriately titled *One Last Thing*. It provides the following best practices to help ensure your success along your polished journey and to keep you moving forward (you'll find more details on each step in the coming pages):

Step 1: Take the pledge . . . know that this journey will require your firm commitment.

Step 2: Set your GPS . . . you know where you want to go, but do you know how to get there?

Step 3: GO . . . press the gas . . . move forward.

Step 4: Encourage your friends to get started . . . you don't have to travel alone. Gather your village and attend or host a Polished Party™.

Step 5: Get the EXTRAS. Get the *Are You Polished? Workbook* designed to be completed individually or by a group of friends during a Polished Party™, as well as the *My Polished Journey Journal* designed to capture the details of your journey and to encourage you to keep moving forward. Visit ThePolishedJourney.com and join our worldwide village of Polished Ladies for support and encouragement, as well as tools and resources that will help you get your polish together.

Step 1: Take the Polished Pledge

Your journey will require commitment and tenacity. The good news is you're worth it! I'm sure you see some form of this pledge every year; however, I made a few updates to reflect the larger scope of your commitment to get yo' polish together.

The Polished Pledge

Please raise your big toes and repeat the following aloud:

- I promise to go to my local nail salon at least once per month and get a real pedicure (even in the winter), or at least pamper myself at home with a full pedicure once a month.

- I promise to keep my polish fresh, intact, and chip-free in between salon visits; I will not cheat by only touching up my big toes.

- I promise to always wear sandals and open-toe shoes that fit. My toes will not hang over or touch the ground, nor will my heels spill over the backs.

- I promise to shave the hairs off my big toes and sand down any mounds of skin before they turn hard and yellow or dark brown.

- I promise to be brutally honest with my girlfriend/ sister/coworker when she asks me if her feet are too ugly to wear sandals or open-toe shoes.

- I promise to support as many women as I can as they get and stay polished.

- I promise to address, manage, and minimize stress to the best of my ability.

- I promise to nurture the feminine spirit within me and obtain emotional stability.

- I promise to spend quality time with myself and learn to fall in love with the real me.

- I promise to be the best physical me I can be.

- I promise to value my relationships, but not more than I value myself.

- I promise to develop the financial acumen needed to take me to the next level.

- I promise to get back on track if I ever get distracted along this journey.

- I promise not to compare my journey to anyone else's journey.

I, _____, on this date of _____, make a solemn promise to myself to get polished and commit to the necessary work to stay polished; I declare and decree that I am worth the effort.

Step 2: Set Your GPS

Okay, quick inventory. You have (a) your vision set, and you know where you're going, and you have (b) commitment to inspire you to get there. Now, you must determine how you're going to get there, so set your GPS. On the following pages, you will find a general *route* for each category. Brainstorm and add what you will unpack, what you will pack, and the steps you will take to propel you forward on your journey.

What should you unpack?

> ONLY TAKE ACTION STEPS
> THAT MOVE YOU FORWARD

Unpack everything and everyone that will hinder you from moving forward or will present a delay in your journey. Say no to and unpack anything that leads to undue stress, such as gossip, wasted time at work, old boyfriends or negative friends, jealousy, procrastination, bad habits, zoning out in front of the television, others' negative opinions of you, too many activities and responsibilities, requests you don't have the time, energy, or desire to take on, and so on.

What should you pack?

Pack anything and anyone that will help you move forward. Pack your Bible, your syllabus, your credit report, your tennis shoes, your juicer, your cardiologist, your personal trainer, your best friends, and so on.

What steps should you take?

Only take action steps that move you forward, of course. Select specific, measurable action steps versus general ones. For example, instead of saying you are going to exercise more, commit to running every Monday, Wednesday, and Friday for

45 minutes. The key is to be as exact and detailed as possible. Then give yourself a specific date to start each of your action steps or a date to complete them.

You may use the strategies already presented in each category; however, your goal is to customize each plan to support your polished vision. It is important to set your GPS and calculate your route by identifying specific actions you will take to move you forward and the specific timeline or date by which you will start or accomplish those actions.

To create action items for each category, brainstorm potential next steps, review your responses to the *Try This* activities and the *Your Perspective* sections, or borrow strategies from the shared stories.

Step 2: Set Your GPS (continued)

What or who do you need to unpack or pack; and what do you need to consistently do in order to acquire the kind of peace and centeredness that can withstand stress and pressure?

EMOTIONAL & SPIRITUAL

Unpack	Pack	Step	Start Date
Regret for what you don't have or what you have yet to accomplish	Words of encouragement, scriptures, sound advice, or other statements to keep you centered and to remind you of your goals (e.g., the polished cards that come with the journal)	Spend 30 minutes a day in prayer or meditation. If a daily goal is not realistic for this season in your life, establish an exact number, and stick to it. For example, 10 minutes, three days a week.	

Step 2: Set Your GPS (continued)

What or who do you need to unpack or pack; and what do you need to consistently do in order to continue to evolve your fabulous YOU? Who do you say that you are?

SELF-IDENTITY

Unpack	Pack	Step	Start Date
'Distracted time' at work (i.e., reading personal emails, taking personal calls, gossip, web surfing, etc.) in order to eliminate the need to spend extra time at work. Instead, gain more time for yourself (perhaps accomplishing some of the things on your Step list).	A list of things you have always wanted to do, that support who you say you are.	Research a cause to which you can volunteer your time, talents, and/ or treasures. Volunteer your time, talents, and/ or treasures.	

Set Your GPS (continued)

What or who do you need to unpack or pack; and what do you need to consistently do in order to acquire and/or maintain your best physical you? What is your personal style saying about you?

PHYSICAL

Unpack	Pack	Step	Start Date
The fear of sweating out your hair.	Courage to say goodbye to your current physical self if there is a better physical you on the horizon. A personal trainer or a committed workout group.	Workout every day for at least 30 minutes. You are worth 30 minutes of your own time, Suga! If you shoot for 7 days a week and only make 4-5 days, you're still golden.	
The fear of going to the doctor.		Schedule a doctor's appointment.	

Set Your GPS (continued)

What or who do you need to unpack or pack; and what do you need to consistently do in order to nurture those relationships that positively support who you say that you are? Do you have a healthy relationship with yourself?

RELATIONAL

Unpack	Pack	Step	Start Date
Neediness and petty grudges. How long are you going to be mad? Your hostility is only hurting you. Every dishonoring relationship. Say goodbye. It only hurts for a little while.	Some honesty. Do you really need 13,375 social network "friends"?	Schedule and host family dinner every 5th Sunday. Spend 90 minutes of quality time with your family (e.g., husband, parents, children, the family matriarch/patriarch, etc.) every week.	

Set Your GPS (continued)

What or who do you need to unpack or pack; and what do you need to consistently do in order to acquire and maintain financial freedom, acumen, and your vision for this category? Are you financially prepared for today *and* tomorrow?

FINANCIAL

Unpack	Pack	Step	Start Date
Daily trips to the coffee house. Sure, that caramel drink is delicious, but is it worth $1825.00? That is how much you could potentially save annually!	Your credit reports.	Save $50.00 each week. Determine how much your weekly bills amount to for a month. Create a budget and stick to it.	

Step 3: GO!

A vision is but a dream if you don't take the necessary action to bring it to fruition. Your GPS is set, and the route has been calculated. Now take the course of action outlined in your GPS (unpack, pack, and step). Start with the category with the lowest score (see page 143) and create a specific start date for each action step (if you haven't already), then work your way through your entire list.

Maintenance is mandatory. Make sure you continue to **work your strategy daily**. Revisit your vision and commitment frequently to minimize delays and the probability of getting off track. Hopefully, it will strengthen your aptitude to refocus when you do. Remember to declare something. Be sure to charge the atmosphere and focus your efforts with daily vision declarations. Along your journey, you will find it necessary to reset your GPS. What else do you need to unpack or pack? What steps were most successful? What additional steps do you need to take? What potholes or detours did you encounter? How did you overcome them?

Step 4: Encourage a Group of Your Friends to Start Their Polished Journey

Hold each other accountable for your collective progress and success. This group should commit to ensuring each woman stays focused, and in the face of perceived failure, is inspired and supported to get back on track. If you commit to others, the probability of success is 65%; setting specific accountability appointments increases your probability to 95%. Don't merely select a group of friends to take on this journey and stop there. Intentionally meet periodically to keep each other on track. Use the questions at the end of this book to help you host your own Polished Party™ or grab a group of your friends and attend a Full-Service Polished Party™ together. You'll have a blast!

Step 5: Get the EXTRAS!

Get the *Are You Polished? Workbook* and the *My Polished Journey Journal* to work through additional experiential activities and to track your progress.

This book is designed to be the foundation of your journey; the strategies found within focus on pampering and setting your GPS. The workbook is designed to be an extended companion, and the strategies it presents focus on creating forward movement in each category and further defining your rhythm. The workbook is an interactive guide that outlines the path and next steps toward nurturing a polished life and can be completed individually, by a group of friends, or during one of our Full-Service Polish Parties™.

Included in the workbook:

- Step by step, sound advice for every category: emotional & spiritual, self-identity, physical, relational, and financial.

- 'Polishing' Activities: experiential exercises that bring the presented advice to life by guiding you as you apply what you've learned.

- Witty insight and quotes that encourage the feminine spirit.

The journal is truly about living life in abundance as you actualize, maintain and nurture your polish. The journal encourages you to capture your emotions, your perceived failures, and most importantly, your successes. The journal comes with:

- Space to set your GPS and to journal your experience.

- Instructions for guided journaling, as well as free-form journaling.

- One set of polished cards to carry the advice, witty insights, and quotes with you or give to your friends to encourage them along their journey.

AFTERWORD
WELL . . . BECAUSE THERE WAS A FOREWORD

PAMPER YOURSELF. FIND YOUR RHYTHM. LIVE LIFE ABUNDANTLY!

From the assessment and the stories, to setting your GPS and mapping out your initial polished journey, I trust you enjoyed *Are You Polished?* More importantly, I hope you agree you're worth the effort necessary to establish a habit of consistently and intentionally pampering yourself.

> YOU ARE FEARFULLY AND WONDERFULLY MADE

At the beginning of this book, I made the bold statement, "Women multitask far more efficiently than men could ever even imagine." I envision every woman reading that statement cheered in agreement. However, the stories told, the presented statistics, and most likely your own testimony support Stanford University's research confirming multitasking is a myth, and far less productive than completing one task at a time. Statistical data that revealed women experience more severe physical and emotional symptoms of stress than men was also presented at the beginning of this book. In fact, the same Stanford study discovered frequent multitaskers perform worse than those who tackle their to-do list one item at a time because they have more trouble organizing their thoughts and sifting out irrelevant information. Multitaskers are ultimately slower at switching from one task to another. Ouch! You cannot do it all. You cannot be everything to everyone. The presence of stress and the lack of polish does not equal crazy (as polished does not translate to perfection), but it may mean you need to find your rhythm and establish a greater sense of stability. You may also need to employ a variety of tools to manage the stress you will inevitably experience. You deserve the commitment it will take to create a life full of joy, peace, and purpose. Take time to pamper yourself and encourage your feminine spirit. Know that you are fearfully and wonderfully made.

Well, what are you waiting for? Look down. Is the hypothesis true or false?

A woman's sanity is directly linked to her pedicure.

Tell me what you think; I want to hear from you. If you want to react to the hypothesis or share your own journey, visit ThePolishedJourney.com.

DISCUSSION QUESTIONS

FOR YOUR OWN POLISHED PARTY™

IS A WOMAN'S SANITY DIRECTLY LINKED TO HER PEDICURE?

Here are a few questions to help bring the stories and the content of this book to life. Work through them alone or host your own Polished Party™ and use these questions to guide your discussion.

THE HYPOTHESIS

1. Is a woman's sanity directly linked to her pedicure? Why or why not?

    *   Discuss evidence/experiences that support the hypothesis.

    *   Discuss evidence/experiences that are contrary to the hypothesis.

2. Are you polished?

- Which polished type do you relate to most often?

- Which polished type are you right now?

- If others had to guess your polished type based on how you have handled stress and behaved lately, how would they describe you?

- Are you too busy to take care of or pamper yourself?

- What does your intentional pampering strategy look like?

3. Consider each of the polished types and discuss the following:

   - High Polished: Who is she really? What is good about being high polished? What is at risk if she remains high polished?

   - Wrecked: What has she lost? When will she recover? What will it take to encourage her to take the first step toward becoming polished?

   - Chipped: What has she dropped along the way? What is the worst part of being/feeling chipped?

   - Layered: Why is she juggling so much? Why is looking the part so important to her? What will happen if she doesn't learn to *unpack* and say no?

   - Polished: How is she juggling it all? Does *polished* mean without flaws or challenges? Is polished attainable; why or why not? What does perfectly polished look like for you?

4. What fundamental changes could you make concerning how you manage stress?

5. What fundamental changes could you make concerning the degree to which you safely put you first?

6. Fill in the blanks:

   - _____ is my strongest polished category.

   - Out of all the polished categories, _____ is my greatest opportunity.

STATISTICALLY SPEAKING

1. Discuss the following statistics from the American Psychological Association:

   - Women are more likely than men (28% vs. 20%) to report having a great deal of stress (8, 9, or 10 on a 10-point scale).

   - Women are more likely to report that money (79% compared with 73% of men) and the economy (68% compared with 61% of men) are sources of great stress.

   - Women are more likely to report physical and emotional symptoms of stress than men, such as having had a headache (41% vs. 30%), having felt as though they could cry (44% vs. 15%), or having had an upset stomach or indigestion (32% vs. 21%).

   - 49% of women have lain awake at night because of stress; only 33% of women report being successful in their efforts to get enough sleep.

   - 35% of women report success in their efforts to manage stress.

- 36% of women report success in their efforts to eat healthily.

- 29% of women report success in their efforts to be physically active.

2. Discuss the following symptoms of stress:

   - Reduced sex drive

   - Irregular periods

   - Acne breakouts

   - Hair loss

   - Poor digestion

   - Depression

   - Insomnia

   - Weight gain

   - Decreased fertility

   - Increased risk of heart disease and stroke

3. What do you think comes first: stress or lack of balance/rhythm?

4. What should be established first: stress management or balance/rhythm?

THE POLISHED JOURNEY

1. What was the most significant *aha* moment you had while reading the entire book? Why?

2. What emotions did you experience as you read through the stories?

3. What one experience stands out to you concerning the stories you read?

4. If given a chance, what would you ask each of the women? (You can ask a different question for each woman.)

    - What question would you ask Patrice? How do you think she would respond? (Email me.)

    - What question would you ask Rebecca? How do you think she would respond?

    - What question would you ask Monique? How do you think she would respond?

    - What question would you ask Nichole? How do you think she would respond?

    - What question would you ask Kelly? How do you think she would respond?

    - What question would you ask Wendy? How do you think she would respond?

    - What question would you ask Debra? How do you think she would respond?

5. What is one personal experience you remembered as you read the stories?

6. What is the most important thing you discovered about yourself *after* reading *Are You Polished?*

YOUR POLISHED JOURNEY

1. What polished category are you working on right now?

2. What will you unpack/what have you unpacked along your journey?

3. What will you pack/what have you packed along your journey?

4. What inspires you the most to move forward?

5. Who in your village inspires you to move forward? How can they support you?

6. How can you inspire your village to move forward with you?

7. What advice would you give other women in a similar situation?

8. Knowing what you know now, what would you tell yourself at the start of your journey?

9. What is your favorite beauty secret?

10. What is your favorite pampering secret?

11. As a woman, what is the best advice you have ever received?

12. Are you polished right now?

13. Is a woman's sanity directly linked to her pedicure? Why or why not?

I Am My Sister/Friend's Keeper

1. What would you like to know from the other women in the group? How they:

   - Pamper themselves?

   - Manage stress?

   - Nurture their emotional and spiritual selves?

   - Strengthen their self-identity?

   - Improve their physical self?

- Enhance their relationships?

- Grow their finances?

2. What did you get out of the book or the group discussions that will help you:

   - Today/tomorrow?

   - Next week?

   - Next month?

3. What will make taking the first (or next) step on your journey the most challenging? How can the group help you overcome this challenge?

REFERENCES
BECAUSE I DIDN'T JUST MAKE THIS STUFF UP

DID YOU KNOW?

American Psychological Association (2015). Retrieved from https://www.apa.org/news/press/releases/stress/2010/gender-stress.aspx

Gregoire, C (2013). "10 Ways Stress Affects Women's Health." The Huffington Post

Google search of *Balance*: an even distribution of weight enabling someone or something to remain upright and steady; a condition in which different elements are equal or in the correct proportions.

Google search of *Rhythm*: a strong, regular, repeated pattern of movement or sound.

PART III: YOUR JOURNEY STARTS HERE

Emotional & Spiritual

Mills, H., Dombeck, M., & Reiss, N. "Mental and Emotional Impact of Stress." Retrieved from https://www.mentalhelp. net/stress/emotional-impact/

Self-Identity

Joo, E., Lee, J., & Choi, K. (2012). "Perceived Stress and Self- esteem Mediate the Effects of Work-related Stress on Depression." Stress and Health; Volume 29, Issue 1, pages 75–81. Retrieved from https://onlinelibrary.wiley.com/doi/ pdf/10.1002/smi.2428

Meier, L., Robins, R., & Orth, U. (2013). "Disentangling the Effects of Low Self-Esteem and Stressful Events on Depression: Findings from Three Longitudinal Studies." Retrieved from http://psychology.usf.edu/faculty/data/lmeier/7.pdf

Orth, U., Robins, R. (2013). "Understanding the Link Between Low Self-Esteem and Depression." Retrieved from https:// journals.sagepub.com/doi/10.1177/0963721413492763

Relational

Bunch, T. (2014). "Stress of Toxic Relationships: A Risk Factor for Heart Disease in Women." Retrieved from https://www. everydayhealth.com/columns/jared-bunch-rhythm-of-life/ stress-toxic-relationships-risk-factor-heart-disease-women/

Google search of *Compassion*: sympathetic pity and concern for the sufferings or misfortunes of others

Financial

Khalfani-Cox, L. (2017). "Zero Debt: The Ultimate Guide to Financial Freedom." Advantage World Press - TheMoneyCoach. net, LLC; 3rd edition

The Hypothesis: The Rundown

Badu, Erykah (2000). "Bag Lady." *Mama's Gun* album

Write the Vision & Make It Plain

Feinstein, A. (2014). "Why You Should Be Writing Down Your Goals." Forbes / Forbes Woman

PART IV: ONE LAST THING

Goal Setting

Oppong, T. (2017). "This is How to Increase the Odds of Reaching Your Goals by 95%." Retrieved from https://medium.com/the-mission/the-accountability- effect-a-simple-way-to-achieve-your-goals-and-boost-your-performance-8a0 7c76ef53a

Multi-tasking

Gorlick, A. (2009). "Media multitaskers pay mental price, Stanford study shows." Retrieved from https://news.stanford.edu/2009/08/24/multitask-research-study-082409/

Mautz, S. (2017). "Psychology and Neuroscience Blow-Up the Myth of Effective Multitasking." Retrieved from https://www.inc.com/scott-mautz/psychology-and-neuroscience-blow-up-th e-myth-of-effective-multitasking.html

ABOUT THE AUTHOR

P atrice L. Harris is a passionate Training and Diversity professional. She is also an Elder in one of the largest and fastest growing ministries in Cleveland/Akron Ohio, a loving wife, a creative author, and a driven CEO of StirUPtheGift, Unlimited! and Perfectly Polished Enterprise, LLC. Both businesses were started with her husband, Michael D. Harris. The Harris' vision of Perfectly Polished Enterprise, LLC has inspired an *Are You Polished?* movement that brings diverse women together and encourages them to pamper themselves, to live life in abundance, and to actively find their rhythm (forward movement) in every aspect of their lives:

- Emotional & Spiritual

- Self-Identity

- Physical

- Relational

- Financial

A militant graduate of Hampton University and a humbled grad alumna of Regent University, Patrice's passion has always been to enjoy life, serve others, and excel in whatever she puts her heart and hands to. Patrice also thinks this section of the book sounds like the homepage of a dating website, not that she would know personally.

Are You Polished?

Here's your Polished Checklist:

- ☐   Take the Assessment – pg. 5
- ☐   Read the Stories – pg. 29
- ☐   Start Your Own Journey – pg. 115
- ☐   Pledge Your Commitment – pg. 159
- ☐   Set Your GPS – pg. 161

You took all the right first steps.
Get the Extras to ensure you
keep moving forward!

Pamper Yourself | Find Your Rhythm | Live Life in Abundance
ThePolishedJourney.com

You Finished the Book – Now, Get Ready for the Adventure!

Your Polished Checklist, continued:

- ☐ GO!
- ☐ Encourage Your Friends to Start Their Journey
- ☐ Take the Free Assessment at ThePolishedJourney.com
- ☐ Get the Extras
  - ▪ The Workbook
  - ▪ The Journal
  - ▪ Join our Worldwide Village of Polished Ladies

Made in the USA
Monee, IL
15 July 2020

35790952R00125